P9-DMU-328

The
PILGRIM'S
PROGRESS

The
PILGRIM'S
PROGRESS

Experience the Spiritual Classic through 40 Days of Daily Devotion

JOHN BUNYAN
WITH HAROLD MYRA

Discovery House.
from Our Daily Bread Ministries

The Pilgrim's Progress: Experience the Spiritual Classic through 40 Days of Daily Devotion

Devotionals © 2018 by Harold Myra
The Pilgrim's Progress updated text by Judith E. Markham and © 1989 by Discovery House
All rights reserved.

Discovery House is affiliated with Our Daily Bread Ministries, Grand Rapids, Michigan.

Requests for permission to quote from this book should be directed to: Permissions Department, Discovery House, PO Box 3566, Grand Rapids, MI 49501, or contact us by email at permissionsdept@dhp.org.

Citations for Bible verses quoted in the book are listed by chapter and in order of appearance at the back of the book. See "List of Scriptures Cited."

Unless otherwise indicated, all Scripture quotations are taken from the Holy Bible, New Living Translation, copyright © 1996, 2004, 2007, 2013 by Tyndale House Foundation. Used by permission of Tyndale House Publishers, Inc., Carol Stream, Illinois 60188. All rights reserved.
    Quotations marked ESV are from The Holy Bible, English Standard Version® (ESV®), copyright © 2001 by Crossway, a publishing ministry of Good News Publishers. Used by permission. All rights reserved.
    Quotations marked GNT are from the Good News Translation, Second Edition. Copyright © 1992 by American Bible Society. Used by permission. All rights reserved.
    Quotations marked KJV are from the King James Version.
    Quotations marked NASB are from the New American Standard Bible®, Copyright © 1960, 1962, 1963, 1968, 1971, 1972, 1973, 1975, 1977, 1995 by The Lockman Foundation. Used by permission.
    Quotations marked NIV are from the Holy Bible, New International Version®, NIV®. Copyright © 1973, 1978, 1984, 2011 by Biblica, Inc.™ Used by permission of Zondervan. All rights reserved worldwide. www.zondervan.com. The "NIV" and "New International Version" are trademarks registered in the United States Patent and Trademark Office by Biblica, Inc. ™
    Quotations marked NKJV are from the New King James Version®. Copyright © 1982 by Thomas Nelson. Used by permission. All rights reserved.

Interior design by Michael J. Williams

ISBN: 978-1-62707-675-3

Printed in the United States of America
First printing in 2018

CONTENTS

INTRODUCTION

The Pilgrim's Progress awakens in some of us childhood memories of reading the classic as an adventure story. We recall those flaming darts and Giant Despair, the swords and monsters, the Beautiful Palace, Vanity Fair, the Delectable Mountains, and, finally, the glories of the Celestial City. As children, we were challenged by its call to resist temptations, fight evil, and wield weapons of faith. Further on in our earthly pilgrimages, we learned how complex life is, and how powerful the lures of temptations. Betrayals and reversals and the world's hostility toward faith can bring dismay and catch us by surprise.

Although the world has changed dramatically since John Bunyan wrote *The Pilgrim's Progress* more than three hundred years ago, some things have remained remarkably unchanged. We continue to face today many of the same struggles God's people have faced for millennia—we are still fighting spiritual battles, wrestling with difficult theological questions, and are often torn by the invisible forces of evil.

Might the vivid images, penetrating truths, and dire warnings of *The Pilgrim's Progress* be just as relevant to our struggles as they were to those in Bunyan's time? Scholars have called Bunyan a genius who created "a humane classic of potent religious depth." It has been described as a great work of creative art, its characterizations and satiric portrayals conveying life with vivid and timeless authenticity. First published in 1678, it has been translated into more than 200 languages and has never been out of print.

Readers across the centuries and decades continue to find Bunyan's imaginative tale both relevant and powerful. Nineteenth-century preacher Charles Spurgeon considered *The Pilgrim's Progress* his most important spiritual resource next to the Bible. For instance, we see its influence in his comment about heaven: "Oh, infinitely better is the end of a spiritual life than the beginning. Contrast the Slough of Despond with the Celestial City and human intellect cannot fail to see how much better, how infinitely better, the end is than the beginning." Author and theologian J. I. Packer read it annually for fifty years, considering it "a classic above all other classics of the Christian life."

The book in your hand is structured in two parts. Part 1 features forty devotional reflections. Each begins with a brief summary of a scene from the pilgrim's story and is then followed by a meditation and a prayer. The citations for quoted scripture passages are included at the back of the book. The full text of *The Pilgrim's Progress* follows the forty devotions in Part 2.

For those who might view Bunyan's allegory as heavy on spiritual warfare and the devil's attacks, this bracing word from Oswald Chambers may apply: "Satan comes in with his temptations, and we are apt to say it is no use to go on. . . . The Christian life is gloriously difficult, but the difficulty of it does not make us faint and cave in, it rouses us up to overcome. . . . Thank God he does give us difficult things to do! His salvation is a glad thing, but it is also a heroic, holy thing. It tests us for all we are worth."

The pilgrim was tested for all he was worth. We, too, are invited to the heroic, holy adventure. When you find yourself in the middle of it, may these daily devotions provide insights and encouragement for the journey.

PART I

THE LIGHT
IN A DARK LAND

The story begins with a man named Christian bearing a great burden on his back and a book in his hand. He is weeping and trembling as he reads of judgment to come. He cries out, "What shall I do?"

His family and neighbors consider him deranged. For days he walks alone in the fields, reading and praying, distraught.

Finally, a man named Evangelist comes toward him and asks why he is crying. He replies he fears judgment and hell and doesn't know what to do or where to go. Evangelist points to a wicket-gate and a shining light in the distance and asks if he sees it.

"I think I do," he says.

"Keep your eyes on that light," Evangelist instructs, "and go directly to it; then you will see the gate. Knock on it, and you will be told what you should do."

Isaiah the prophet, seeing the grandeur and holiness of God, cried out, "Woe is me, for I am undone! Because I am a man of unclean lips, and I dwell in the midst of a people of unclean lips." Bunyan's pilgrim, reading the holy book, likewise cried out, trembling, and wept for his sins.

As in the City of Destruction, so in our culture, the holiness of God and our need for repentance and reconciliation seldom surface. We live out our days in a world that includes injustice, hypocrisy, degradation, and despair. Yet the Holy Book is always available to each of us, revealing the mysteries of God's grandeur and holiness.

Despite Isaiah's woe and sense of being undone, he prophesied hope: "The people who walk in darkness will see a great light; those who live in a dark land, the light will shine on them."

Centuries later, Matthew described the beginning of Jesus's ministry by quoting Isaiah this way: "The people living in darkness have seen a great light; on those living in the land of the shadow of death, a light has dawned."

Evangelist told Christian, "Keep your eyes on that light."

When we live in a world rife with crises and distress, we may well sense we are walking in a dark land, needing light far brighter and more authentic than anything the flickering colors and images on our screens can provide. It is still true that Jesus is the light of the world, and we are all pilgrims. The light shines for all of us, and we are invited to look for it, go to it, and to knock at the gate.

Isaiah compels us to action with another challenge: "Arise, shine, for your light has come, and the glory of the LORD rises upon you." What a sobering, magnificent picture of the celestial light in our darkness. Let us keep our eyes on that light.

Lord, the longer I live, the more I realize how much I fall short of your purity and love. Please help me this day to seek you where you can be found, to listen for your instructions, and to keep my eyes fixed on the light you give.

"NONSENSE!"

Seeing the light in the distance, Christian ran toward it. But his family and his neighbors called for him to come back.

Two men—one named Obstinate and the other named Pliable—resolved to bring him back by force and pursued him. When they caught up, Christian asked them, "Why have you come?"

"To persuade you to go back with us," they said.

But Christian warned them he was fleeing impending fire and judgment on their city.

"Nonsense!" Obstinate declared, and called him a crazy fool.

Pliable objected and said to Obstinate, "Don't be unkind. If what the good Christian says about the things he seeks is true, I am inclined go with him."

Obstinate then called Pliable a fool, and went back to the City of Destruction. But Pliable joined Christian, and they continued to talk as they headed toward the light.

In his letter to the church at Ephesus, the apostle Paul writes the following description of people who ignore God: "They are darkened in their understanding and separated from the life of God . . . due to the hardening of their hearts. . . . They have given themselves over to sensuality so as to indulge every kind of impurity, and they are full of greed."

It's a portrayal that also accurately describes Christian's neighbors and family. And in our own time, we don't have to look far to see dispiriting examples of the same. However, Paul also gives us this good news: "Because of his great love for us, God, who is rich in mercy, made us alive with Christ even when we were dead in transgressions."

Good News indeed.

Yet we who have welcomed God's Holy Spirit into our lives still struggle, and we often wrestle with the tensions of trying to "hate what is wrong" and simultaneously "hold tightly to what is good." This is especially hard to do in a world that seems instead to love what is wrong and hold tightly to what is bad. We find ourselves saddened by the impact this has on the innocent and on all of us.

Just as Obstinate did, many today believe sinfulness and responding to God's mercy is religious kill-joy nonsense. Yet the energizing truth is that God is the source of all good gifts and the source of joy. If God does not permit something, it is only because it leads to despair and ruin, just as Bunyan portrays it in the City of Destruction.

Jesus came that we might have life and "have it to the full." Christian fled the City of Destruction out of fear, but he also fled *toward* something—toward light and grace and joy.

Father in heaven, how easy it is for me to look around at all that distresses me and to be anxious about what's happening—and even more anxious about what may happen. I confess that sometimes my worries and fears triumph over my faith. Please help me to focus instead on the light and grace and joy you promise. Lead me, this day and every day, on the paths of love and righteousness.

YOU CALL THIS "HAPPINESS"?

As he walked with Pliable, Christian described the wonders and delights of salvation and heaven. "We will be given crowns of glory," Christian said, "and garments that will make us shine like the sun." All tears would be wiped from their eyes. Angels would dazzle them, and no one would be unkind, for all would be loving and holy.

Pliable was inspired! Unlike Christian, he had no burden on his back, and he said, "Let's hurry."

Yet, before long, they fell into a bog called the Swamp of Despond. There, they floundered in the mud.

"Is this the happiness you've been telling me about?" Pliable angrily exclaimed. When he at last succeeded in freeing himself from the muck and the mire, Pliable left Christian there and returned to the City of Destruction.

Christian had plenty of encouraging news to share with Pliable as they walked along. He quoted the blessed book, perhaps including psalms full of praise for God's wonders and the gospel accounts of angels announcing the greatest story ever told.

Initially, Pliable listened eagerly and was cheered by Christian's descriptions of their destination—a kingdom of everlasting life where there would be no more crying or sorrow. But what happened next parallels an experience many of us have on the walk of faith. One moment we're rejoicing on a spiritual mountaintop, and the next moment we're slogging through a spiritual swamp.

Pliable is an example of how *not* to deal with life's reversals and hardships.

Unlike Christian, he carried no burden on his back. He was unaware he was shallow and desperately needy, with no sense of his own sin or the ways he fell short of God's glory. He was unable to grasp the Good News, for he felt he had no need for it. Pliable liked what he heard about heaven and the rewards to come, but he had no understanding of his true spiritual condition. As a result, he didn't realize how close he was to salvation. He failed to heed the call the prophet Isaiah issues to all of us: "Seek the LORD while you can find him. Call on him now while he is near. Let the wicked change their ways and banish the very thought of doing wrong. Let them turn to the LORD that he may have mercy on them. Yes, turn to our God, for he will forgive generously."

Because Pliable hadn't reckoned with his fallen condition, he had no idea what he was walking away from. But Christian did. He was determined to seek the Lord and to keep struggling across the swamp toward the light.

❧

Holy and Almighty God, help me to see my true condition as you see it. Give me strength to change my ways and to banish even the thought of doing wrong. I believe with my whole heart that your love is so great you sent your Son to this troubled world to redeem me. Help me not to fall back into old patterns, but in my struggles, to call on you in the expectation that you will shower me with mercy and lead me closer to your light.

FLOUNDERING IN THE SWAMP

Although Pliable managed to free himself from the muck, Christian continued to struggle in the Swamp of Despond. Eventually, he made his way to the side of the swamp nearest the wicket-gate, but he couldn't get out because of the burden on his back.

Finally, a man named Help came along and asked, "What are you doing there?"

"Sir," Christian said, "I was told to go this way by a man called Evangelist, who directed me also to yonder gate, . . . and as I was going toward it, I fell in here."

"But why did you not look for the steps?" asked Help.

Christian admitted he had been so afraid that he wasn't paying attention.

"Give me your hand," said Help. Then he drew Christian up to firm ground and told him to go on his way.

⚬✖⚬

Why was Christian stuck in the Swamp of Despond? Because he was so caught up in his own concerns, he didn't pay attention to where he was going. He missed the steps that would have kept him out of the miry bog.

When we're on autopilot—caught up in our own worries, forgetting to search the Word, and deaf to the whispers of the Holy Spirit—it's inevitable that we will lose our way. Sooner or later, we will blindly stumble into the Swamp of Despond. And even when we're prayerful and trying to follow God's leading, life's disappointments and tragedies can still crush our spirits and leave us floundering.

However it is we end up in the swamp, the words of Scripture always provide solid steps through the muck and quicksands of life. "Your word is a lamp to guide my feet and a light for my path," writes the psalmist. Taken from Psalm 119, the longest in the book of Psalms, it is but one of many verses that celebrate how valuable and wonderful God's instructions are. In the New Testament, the apostle Paul echoes this same theme when he writes, "All Scripture is inspired by God and is useful to teach us what is true and to make us realize what is wrong in our lives. It corrects us when we are wrong and teaches us to do what is right."

Like Christian, we may find ourselves floundering and despondent at some point on our journey. Scripture provides stability and guidance, and reaching out to others for help can pull us onto solid ground. We might reach out to a friend or family member, a pastor or small group leader, a Christian counselor, or a medical professional. "Share each other's burdens," writes the apostle Paul. That means we seek and graciously receive assistance when we need it, and then offer assistance to others when they need it. Sometimes we need Help to give us a hand, and other times we become Help for a fellow struggler.

Holy Spirit of God, I remember that Jesus said to his disciples you would come as our helper, and I need your presence and your help. Please be with me today. Show me how to help others who struggle. And when I feel my feet sinking in weariness and discouragement, help me to shift my focus from my difficulties to your goodness and your wonderful works.

"WHY THROW YOUR LIFE AWAY?"

Walking along toward the light, Christian spied Mr. Worldly Wiseman walking toward him. When their paths crossed, the worldly man asked the pilgrim, "Where are you going in this burdened manner?"

"To yonder wicket-gate . . . to get rid of my heavy burden," Christian replied.

Mr. Worldly Wiseman advised him to get rid of it quickly.

Christian replied that was exactly what he wanted, but he couldn't remove the burden by himself. He explained that Evangelist had sent him this way to get rid of his burden.

"I condemn him for his advice," Worldly Wiseman said, "for there is no more dangerous and troublesome way . . . for I see the dirt of the Swamp of Despond upon you. . . . If you continue on, you are likely to meet with weariness, pain, hunger, perils, nakedness, sword, lions, dragons, darkness, and, in a word, death! . . . So why should you carelessly throw your life away on the word of a stranger?"

But Christian said the burden on his back was more terrible than all those things.

⁓

Years ago, a beer commercial trumpeted, "You only go around once in life, so go for all the gusto you can." Does beer provide gusto? How about all the other products endlessly hawked in our ad-saturated society? Do they satisfy? Probably not. And yet, from marketers, and from the lips of Mr. Worldly Wiseman, we hear the endless refrain, "Why throw your life away? Go for the gusto!"

Jesus counters with a different message: "If you cling to your life, you will lose it; but if you give up your life for me, you will find it." Or, in the words of pastor Rick Warren, "It's not about you." If you want a life of meaning and purpose, you won't find it in going for the gusto, or in any other self-indulgent pursuits Mr. Worldly Wiseman might advise.

Proverbs, the Bible's book of wisdom, repeatedly warns us to stay away from bad advice, including our own:

"Stay away from fools, for you won't find knowledge on their lips."

"Fools make fun of guilt, but the godly acknowledge it and seek reconciliation."

"There is a path before each person that seems right, but it ends in death."

In our age of information glut, finding true wisdom requires both effort and discernment. Most important, it requires the guidance of the Holy Spirit. The world's wisdom beckons us to cling to our life—to avoid any path on which we might encounter pain or perils. The Lord beckons us instead to give up our life for him, which is precisely what Mr. Worldly Wiseman considered the worst advice of all. But it is in staying on that path toward the light that we are freed from our burdens and discover the meaningful life we seek.

Lord, grant me wisdom today as I seek to live by your guidance. In a world that promotes self-centeredness and cynicism, help me to choose the path of loving self-sacrifice. Give me the strength I need to continue, even when I experience weariness, pain, hunger, and perils. Make me an instrument of your peace. Keep my feet firmly planted on your path of life and purpose.

SHORTCUT TO THE HAPPY LIFE

The solution is at hand," Mr. Worldly Wiseman assured Christian, "and it does not involve those dangers."

Here was the plan he described: "In that village over there called Morality lives a gentleman named Legality . . . who has the skill to help men rid themselves of burdens such as yours. . . . His handsome young son, Civility, can help you as well. . . . You may send for your wife and children to join you in this village. . . . Everything you need for a happy life will be provided there."

Christian listened and found his suggestions very appealing. He turned and headed for Mr. Legality's house. However, he soon came to a very steep hill. As he climbed it, his burden felt heavier than ever before. Then he saw flashes of fire coming out of the hill!

Christian began sweating and quaking with fear, and he was sorry he had taken Mr. Worldly Wiseman's counsel. That's when he saw Evangelist coming to meet him, and he blushed with shame.

"What are you doing here, Christian?" Evangelist asked.

Christian was speechless.

"Didn't I tell you the way to the little wicket-gate?"

Christian confessed that after floundering in the Swamp of Despond, a man had persuaded him that he could more quickly be rid of his burden if he were to leave the path and go a different way.

The steep hill Christian found so difficult and frightening is Mount Sinai, the place where Moses received the Law from God. The writer of Hebrews describes Mount Sinai this way: "A place of flaming fire, darkness, gloom, and whirlwind," where the Israelites heard "an awesome trumpet blast and a voice so terrible that they begged God to stop speaking. . . . Moses himself was so frightened at the sight that he said, 'I am terrified and trembling.'"

Mr. Worldly Wiseman's counsel to consult Legality—to live by the law—led Christian to a painful realization: he was incapable of climbing Legality's hill. In other words, he couldn't live up to the demands of the law—none of us can. When we measure ourselves by God's standards, we fall far, far short and our burdens become only heavier and harder to bear.

Christian learned he couldn't be rid of his burden and find happiness by trying to climb Mount Sinai. But he could return to the path Evangelist had shown him—the path to the gate, which led to authentic happiness.

The writer of Hebrews contrasts the insurmountable Mount Sinai with yet another mountain: "You have come to Mount Zion," the writer proclaims, "to the city of the living God, the heavenly Jerusalem, and to countless thousands of angels in a joyful gathering." Ah! This is where true joy is found! The writer concludes, "Since we are receiving a Kingdom that is unshakable, let us be thankful and please God by worshiping him with fear and awe. For our God is a devouring fire."

When we worship God in fear and awe, we need not fear the flames of Sinai as we follow his path of joy and light to the Celestial City.

Thank you, Lord, for all you have done for me. I am so grateful that I can come to you through the grace and joy of Mount Zion rather than the fire and gloom of Mount Sinai. I ask your guidance this day so I can keep to the right paths and complete the tasks you have for me. Thank you for your love and for making a place for me in your joyful, unshakable Kingdom.

"STRAIT IS THE GATE"

Evangelist, finding Christian had left the path to climb the hill to Legality's house, showed him the error of his ways and said, "The just shall live by faith. . . . You have begun to reject the counsel of the Most High and to draw back from the way of peace."

Christian fell at his feet, crying, "Woe is me, for I am undone!"

Evangelist took him by the hand and explained how Mr. Worldly Wiseman's counsel had put him on the path that leads to death.

"You must abhor his turning you out of the way," Evangelist warned, "because to do this is to reject the counsel of God for the counsel of a Worldly Wiseman. The Lord says, 'Strive to enter in at the strait gate,' the gate to which I sent you, for 'strait is the gate that leadeth unto life, and few there be that find it.'"

Christian cursed the moment he had met Mr. Worldly Wiseman. He called himself a fool and asked Evangelist if there was any hope for him.

"Your sin is very great," Evangelist replied, "you have forsaken the way that is good and you have taken forbidden paths. Yet the man at the gate will receive you, for he has goodwill for men."

Evangelist quoted Jesus's statement about the narrow gate: "You can enter God's Kingdom only through the narrow gate," Jesus said. "The highway to hell is broad, and its gate is wide for the many who choose that way. But the gateway to life is very narrow and the road is difficult, and only a few ever find it."

The Pilgrim's Progress tells hard stories of spiritual warfare and confronting evil, just as Jesus told hard truths about the road to hell. Yet Jesus is also the supreme example of sacrificial love. The first Bible verse most children memorize in church is this: "For this is how God *loved* the world: He gave his one and only Son, so that everyone who believes in him will not perish but have eternal life." And Jesus said to his followers, "Your love for one another will prove to the world that you are my disciples."

In our day of sound bites and shallow talk, of anger and tribalism, talking about the "strait gate" is uncomfortable for some and offensive to others. Many ridicule the narrow path of faith and love. In such an environment, it's easy to become worn down, making it harder to resist the temptation of an easier path or more enticing opportunity.

Christian was eager to get back on the path to the narrow gate. His ready contrition and teachability are models for our response when we realize we've been wandering. Evangelist acknowledged the seriousness of Christian's offense, but he affirmed that the man at the gate would welcome him. That's a promise we can rely on as well. When we turn and seek God's guidance and follow the whispers of his Spirit, we know we will be welcomed at the gate that leads to life.

Father in heaven, please help me to stay on your path and to stay alert to ways I am tempted to wander. Enlighten my thinking and refresh my spirit. Help me to obey, even when I am confused and weary. Help me to be listening for your voice and obedient to your guidance. And may you be praised for all your wonderful works and care.

KNOCK, AND IT SHALL BE OPENED

Christian finally arrived at the gate, and he found written over it, "Knock, and it shall be opened unto you."

He knocked several times, hoping he would be granted admittance and that God would love him and forgive his sins.

At last, a man named Goodwill appeared, asking who was there, where he had come from, and what he wanted.

"I am a poor burdened sinner," Christian replied. "I come from the City of Destruction, but I am going to Mount Zion so I may be delivered from the wrath to come. . . . I want to know if you are willing to let me in."

"I am willing with all my heart," said Goodwill. Then he opened the gate and quickly pulled him in, explaining that demonic cohorts from Beelzebub's castle shoot arrows at those who come up to the gate.

<hr>

Having escaped the perils of the Swamp of Despond, Mr. Worldly Wiseman's bad advice, and the impossibly steep climb to the house of Legality, Christian sets a straight and swift path to the wicket-gate.

And yet he doesn't realize that he is still in danger, that even as he nears his destination, the evil minions of Beelzebub, a prince of demons, are targeting him. They aim their arrows of doubt, lies, and fear at all who approach the gate, hoping to kill them before they can enter in.

Fortunately, Christian's humility and contrition grant him swift entry through the gate. Bunyan's marginal note reads, "The gate will be opened to brokenhearted sinners."

Throughout our lives, we experience many things that break our hearts, including our own sins, failures, and mistakes. Like Christian, when we are under conviction of sin and keenly aware of our need for the Savior, we knock hard at the gate. And when our spirits are crushed by sorrow, we lean into the promise of Scripture that "the LORD is close to the brokenhearted; he rescues those whose spirits are crushed." Whenever we are brokenhearted, we have a refuge in God.

This scene from *The Pilgrim's Progress* is a vivid reminder that we have an enemy, one who is positioned to crush our spirits and do us harm, especially when we are vulnerable. Whether or not we are aware of it, the devil is aiming at us with fiery arrows, the kind tipped with festering doubts, fears, and falsehoods. "He has always hated the truth," Jesus said of the devil, "because there is no truth in him. . . . He is a liar and the father of lies."

The apostle Paul admonishes us to take the devil's tactics seriously and to protect ourselves. "Put on all of God's armor," he writes, "so that you will be able to stand firm against all the strategies of the devil." After describing the belt of truth, the body armor of God's righteousness, and the shoes of peace, Paul writes, "In addition to all of these, hold up the shield of faith to stop the fiery arrows of the devil."

We don't have to succumb to the enemy's tactics. Our broken-heartedness over sin, the truths of Scripture, and our shield of faith will protect us. Let us pray for the strength to put on the whole armor of God so we can stand firm.

Almighty Father, I don't know how the devil may be targeting me, but I pray for your protection from his temptations and lies. You know his strategies, and you can blunt his attempts to take me down. Please protect me, and help me to serve only you.

GOODWILL AND GRACE

Goodwill then showed Christian the straight and narrow way he should go, the way formed by the patriarchs, prophets, Christ, and his apostles. Christian asked if Goodwill would help him take the burden off his back, but he was told to bear it till he came to the place of deliverance. There, it would fall off by itself.

Goodwill said he should next visit Interpreter, who would show him excellent things.

Interpreter welcomed Christian into his house and showed him the picture of a man with eyes lifted to heaven. The best of books was in his hand.

Then Interpreter showed him a dusty room which, when swept by a man, filled the air with dust so thick Christian nearly choked on it. At Interpreter's direction, a young woman came into the room and sprinkled it with water. Then it was swept and cleansed.

Interpreter explained that the room was the heart of one "who was never sanctified by the sweet grace of the gospel." The dust was original sin. The man who first swept was the Law, which had no power to subdue sin. The young woman who sprinkled the room with water showed "the sweet and precious influence of the gospel."

Life without grace. What's that like? In our story, it's like being in a room full of dust so thick it chokes you. When we try to clean things up, to sweep away our failures with good behavior and heroic self-effort, we're only stirring up the dust of sin by living under the law. What we need instead are the cleansing waters of grace, "the sweet and precious influence of the gospel."

How greatly our world needs grace! Daily we see reports of religious hatred, debauchery, wars, murders of innocents, and despair. We wonder how to live with authentic faith in this world.

What is the sweet grace of the gospel, and how does it relate to our troubles? Consider the following anchor points the Bible reveals about grace.

"We have seen his glory, the glory of the one and only Son, who came from the Father, full of grace and truth." Jesus brings us hope, and he reveals the love and glory of the Father.

"For the grace of God has appeared that offers salvation to all people." The good news, the gospel, is for everyone, everywhere in our fallen world.

"My grace is sufficient for you, for my power is made perfect in weakness." When we feel overwhelmed by our troubles, we can call on the Lord for his strength and grace.

Scripture also gives us this encouragement: "Let us come boldly to the throne of our gracious God. There we will receive his mercy, and we will find grace to help us when we need it most."

Like Christian, we are on a journey through rugged challenges. We are all in great need of grace, and we are invited to humbly seek it from our heavenly Father.

Father in heaven, thank you that I am not under the law but under grace. Help me to believe it, to soak in the reality of your great grace and your love for me. Help me to draw near to you, to receive with gratitude the grace that is made perfect in my weakness. Teach me to be a grace-giver, to extend to others the sweet grace you have lavished on me.

THE WISER CHILD

After the cleansing of the dusty room, Interpreter took Christian "into a little room where sat two little children, each one in his chair." The children were named Passion and Patience.

Passion seemed discontented, but when given a bag of treasure, he rejoiced. He spent it right away and laughed scornfully at Patience, who waited. But it wasn't long until he had spent it all and was left with nothing but rags.

Interpreter explained that Passion represented those who must have it all now—in this world. The saying that a bird in the hand is worth two in the bush has more authority with them than the promises of heaven. At the end of the world, they will have nothing left except rags.

"I see that Patience was wiser in many ways," said Christian, "First, because he waits for the best things. And second, because he will have glory when the other has nothing but rags."

"And you may add another," said Interpreter, "the glory of the next world will never wear out, whereas the good things of this world are suddenly gone."

⧉

Passion and Patience are opposites. In fact, Passion might just as well have been named Impatience. Impatience expresses itself in a range of emotions, but especially in hostility toward any obstacle that comes between a person and his or her desires. Unfettered passion puts what-I-want above everything else. Patience, on the other hand, isn't overly frustrated by obstacles because it takes the long view. Patience is what enables us to attain and enjoy our highest aspirations. Whether we are training, studying, practicing, or working to overcome an obstacle to our goals, it all takes patience.

Patience is fueled by hope, and it is content to wait for the best rather than settle for the immediate. Hope is a strange thing. It is only possible to have hope when what we hope for is not a certainty. "Hope that is seen is no hope at all," writes the apostle Paul. "Who hopes for what they already have? But if we hope for what we do not yet have, we wait for it patiently."

As his journey continues, Christian will need lots of hope, just as we all do when navigating life's rough realities. That is why the apostle Paul encourages us with these words: "We rejoice in our sufferings, knowing that suffering produces endurance, and endurance produces character, and character produces hope, and hope does not put us to shame, because God's love has been poured into our hearts through the Holy Spirit."

When we are caught between passion and patience, when we're tempted to settle for the immediate rather than wait for the best, let us remember that patience is one of the fruits of the Holy Spirit. It's nestled in with love and joy and peace. Patience blended with hope in God's promises keeps us in step with the Spirit.

Holy Spirit of God, teach me to be patient in hope, to keep my eyes at all times on your glory. Pour your love into my heart and

your patience into my character. When I am suffering, help me to rejoice, knowing that you will use it to produce endurance, character, and hope in me.

FIRE, OIL, AND THE DEVIL

Interpreter showed Christian a fire burning against a wall. Someone standing by it kept casting water on it to quench it. But the fire only burned higher and hotter. How could that be?

"The fire is the work of grace in the heart," Interpreter explained. "He who casts water upon it, trying to extinguish it, is the Devil. But let me show you why the fire continues to burn higher and hotter."

Interpreter then took Christian around to the backside of the wall. There he saw a man with a vessel of oil in his hand, which he secretly cast into the fire.

"This is Christ," Interpreter explained, "who, continually, with the oil of his grace, maintains the work begun in the heart. . . . It is hard for the tempted to see how his work of grace is maintained in the soul."

As we determine to follow God's path and to live in the grace and empowering of the Spirit, we can be mystified by what a dynamic, frustrating, marvelous adventure it is. The image Bunyan paints resonates for many of us—the devil and Christ battling in our souls, the evil angel pouring on his nasty flow of temptations and disbelief, dampening our fires of obedience and courage, while at the same time Christ continually fuels our faith.

The conflict within us is always there, changing in specifics, but raging all through our earthly journey, as we will see in the pilgrim's experiences to come.

Christians who live in the midst of military conflict and war often have particular insights into this battle that rages in the heart of every believer. During World War II, German pastor and theologian Helmut Thielicke defied the Nazi regime by continuing to courageously preach the gospel. He had a keen understanding of how the battle between good and evil played out across the human heart. "We are not masters at all," he said, "we are only battlefields between the real masters. The question we face is whether we want to be the child of one, or the slave of the other."

Both Thielicke and his theological predecessor, Martin Luther, emphasized the biblical reality that God and Satan are in a battle for our souls. Luther stressed that God works in the lives of his people even when we can't see what his plans might be. "God won't lie to me or deceive me," he preached, "though at times, nothing in life will seem to make sense."

When we recognize our deep need, when we live in prayerful expectation, heaven is opened to us. Thielicke preached, "He who dares to live this way will wait with the joyful expectancy of a child for the Father's surprises. God is always positive. He makes all things new."

Lord, sometimes it seems like the dark waters of the enemy have all but extinguished the fires of obedience and trust within me.

Thank you for fighting for me, for continually pouring the oil of grace into my soul. Please fuel my faith this day. Help me to resist temptation, and strengthen me for the challenges ahead.

THE DETERMINED, THE DESPAIRING, AND THE TREMBLING

Interpreter led Christian to the door of a stately palace. Persons clothed in gold walked on its roof. Near the door of the palace sat a man at a table, with a book and a pen before him. Also at the doorway were many men who wanted to go in, but dared not. They were afraid of the armed guards who were intent on hurting any who attempted to enter.

But then a strong and determined-looking man approached the man who sat at the table and said, "Set down my name, sir." He then drew his sword, put a helmet on his head, and rushed the armed men. He hacked fiercely and pressed his way into the palace. There, he was welcomed by those who walked atop of the palace, and he was given golden clothes like theirs.

Interpreter then led Christian to a very dark room where a man sat in an iron cage of despair. He had sinned against the light of the Word and the goodness of God. Having despised the spirit of grace, he was beyond repentance and caged in eternal misery.

Next, Interpreter and Christian went to a chamber where a man was rising from bed. As he dressed, he shook and trembled. When Christian asked the reason for the trembling, the man explained that he dreamed that night of fearful thunder and lightning, a great sound of a trumpet, the heavens aflame, and a voice saying, "Arise, ye dead, and come to judgment." Rocks were torn apart, graves opened, and the dead arose—some gladly looked up, others tried to hide. In his dream, the man saw many carried away into the clouds, but he was left behind.

Christian said to Interpreter that these images gave him both hope and fear.

"Keep all these things in mind," Interpreter said, "that they may prod you forward in the way you must go. . . . May the Comforter always be with you, good Christian, to guide you in the way that leads to the City."

Interpreter showed Christian these sobering, bracing scenes—a courageous man of faith, another beyond repentance, and a third left behind at the Judgment—to equip him spiritually for the battles and captivities to come. They were vivid tableaus of caution to help Christian understand the high stakes of his choices, and to keep him moving forward on his journey.

What might we face?

We hear much these days about people's fears in our globalized, polarized world. Some day, we may personally experience disasters such as those we see daily on news reports. Whatever is ahead of us, we know our spiritual resilience will be tested.

On his pilgrimage, Christian faced many of the same seductions and dark worldviews we are confronted with today. It's "the world, the flesh, and the devil." Yet we deal with the old challenges in new forms, including secularism's rise to power, online tribes hostile to Christian values, and the power of pornography just one click away.

Whatever our theological views of a man beyond repentance and another left behind, the core message to take away from Interpreter's three men is that what we believe and what we do have eternal consequences. *The Pilgrim's Progress* is all about taking seriously our brief journey in life, responding to both the assurances and the warnings of the Holy Spirit.

The apostle Paul writes, "Those who are dominated by the sinful nature think about sinful things, but those who are controlled by the Holy Spirit think about things that please the Spirit. So letting your sinful nature control your mind leads to death. But letting the Spirit control your mind leads to life and peace."

Father in heaven, I want to take my life seriously, and to follow the examples of those who respond to challenges and temptations with courage and strength. Teach me, Lord, to consider my ways, allowing both hope and holy fear to lead me forward this day and every day.

THE PLACE OF DELIVERANCE

Christian came to a hill on which stood a cross, and at the bottom a sepulcher or tomb.

As he approached the cross, his burden was loosened from his shoulders and fell from his back. The burden tumbled down until it fell into the sepulcher and was seen no more.

Christian said with a merry heart, "He has given me rest through his sorrow, and life through his death." Tears streamed down his cheeks.

Three Shining Ones came to him and said, "Peace to you." Then each one helped him. The first said, "Your sins are forgiven." The second stripped Christian of his rags and clothed him with a clean garment. The third placed a mark on his forehead and gave him a roll with a seal on it, which he was to look at as he continued his journey, and hand in at the Celestial Gate.

Christian jumped for joy and went on his way singing, "Blest cross! Blest sepulcher! Blest rather be the Man that there was put to shame for me!"

Free of his burden at last and blessed by angels, it's no wonder that Christian sang and jumped for joy. In his exuberance, we might well imagine him singing a full-throated rendition of that catchy Sunday-school tune, "I've got the joy, joy, joy, joy down in my heart . . . down in my heart to stay."

Our individual experiences of approaching the cross and making peace with God may or may not resemble Christian's experience. For some, it includes exuberance, and for others simply a settled peace. For some, it happens over time in a long, slow process, while for others, salvation is an abrupt and unexpected wonder. However it happens, it is a marvel to be freed of our burdens and beloved by God!

Whether or not we've experienced that sort of joy, few of us feel such spiritual bounce continuing day after day. "Down in our hearts" the joy may be, but troubles and our very human failures intrude. For instance, if we meet with Giant Despair, as Christian does later on in his adventures, that catchy song won't exactly apply.

Yet joy is one of the fruits of the Holy Spirit. Isn't the Spirit always with us?

Although our emotions may rise and fall for countless reasons, the apostle Paul tells us that, no matter what our condition, "the Holy Spirit helps us in our weakness." He then adds this stunning description: "The Holy Spirit prays for us with groanings that cannot be expressed in words." When Giant Despair has us by the throat and we don't feel the joy, the Holy Spirit prays for us. That's when we cling to the bedrock joy of knowing God loves us no matter what.

A quote from A. W. Tozer gives us much to ponder: "What I am anxious to see in Christian believers is a beautiful paradox. I want to see in them the joy of finding God while at the same time they are blessedly pursuing him. I want to see in them the great joy of having God yet always wanting him."

Tozer's words blend with this encouragement from the apostle Paul: "May the God of hope fill you with all joy and peace in believing, so that by the power of the Holy Spirit you may abound in hope."

Thank you, Lord, for the gift of salvation. Thank you for releasing me from the burden of my guilt. When my emotions soar, and when they plummet, please help me to rest in the assurance of your love and grace. Rekindle in me the joy of my salvation, and let me today share in Christian's exuberance at being freed of my burdens.

PREY FOR THE ROARING LION

Christian went on joyfully until he came upon three men fast asleep, with chains on their feet. Their names were Simple, Sloth, and Presumption.

"Awake," he shouted at them, "and come away; and if you are willing, I will help you take off your shackles." He also warned them, "If he that goes about like a 'roaring lion' comes by, certainly you will become prey for him."

"I see no danger," said Simple.

"Let me sleep a little more," said Sloth.

"I can make it myself without any help from you!" said Presumption.

And all three went back to sleep.

Christian went on his way, but he was troubled that men in such danger would reject his warning and his kindness in offering to help them remove their chains.

Christian's reference to a roaring lion is drawn from the words of the apostle Peter. "Stay alert!" writes the apostle. "Watch out for your great enemy, the devil. He prowls around like a roaring lion, looking for someone to devour." Peter is writing to mature Christians going through very hard times. He advises them to maintain their faith as they go through fiery trials, to keep on doing right, and to trust in the Lord who created them. "Give all your worries and cares to God," he urges, "for he cares for you."

How do we become prey for the devil? By following the likes of Simple, Sloth, and Presumption. These heedless fellows remind us of cartoon characters who, about to be knocked over cliffs, look at the camera and say the D word: "Duh." They're oblivious to what is about to happen to them.

We can be oblivious to all sorts of sneaky ways the devil tries to infiltrate our lives—including his endless presentations on glowing screens. And when our lives are full of disappointments and suffering, we can focus on our difficult circumstances instead of on God's love and purpose for our lives.

Peter's counsel bears repeating: "Stay alert! Watch out for your great enemy, the devil. He prowls around like a roaring lion, looking for someone to devour. Stand firm against him, and be strong in your faith. Remember that your Christian brothers and sisters all over the world are going through the same kind of suffering you are."

Lord, give me eyes to see my chains—those blind spots that leave me vulnerable to the enemy. Help me not to be lulled into passive acceptance of what draws me away from your guidance and your presence. Keep me alert to what you want to do in my life, and I will praise you for your wonderful works.

A SHORTCUT
OVER THE WALL

Continuing his journey, Christian spied two men tumbling over the wall of the narrow way. They hurried to catch up to him. Their names were Formalist and Hypocrisy.

"We were born in the land of Vain-glory," they said, "and we are going to Mount Zion for the purpose of doing a praiseworthy thing."

When Christian asked why they had climbed the wall rather than entering at the gate, they said their countrymen considered it too far. For more than a thousand years, it had been the custom of their people to take the shortcut.

"You came in at the gate, and we came tumbling over the wall," they said. "In what way is your condition better than ours?"

"I walk by the rule of my Master," Christian said, "You walk by the ignorant working of your own imagination." Whereas they would be considered thieves for not coming in by the door, the Lord would know him by the coat on his back, the mark on his forehead, and the scroll he could read on the way and use to gain admittance at the Celestial Gate.

They gave him no reply, but they looked at each other and laughed.

Christian walked on just ahead of them, reading the scroll the Shining Ones had given him.

When the three of them came to the Hill Difficulty, there was a spring and three paths to choose from—one to the left, one to the right, and one straight up the hill. Christian refreshed himself with a drink from the spring, and then began to ascend the hill on the narrow path straight ahead called Difficulty.

Put off by the steepness of the narrow path, Christian's fellow travelers looked for other paths. One took the path called Danger, and the other took the path called Destruction.

Formalist and Hypocrisy have something in common: they both find ways to avoid responding to God's initiatives. Those who are formalists take comfort and pride in performing religious rituals, but they're not listening for the voice of the Holy Spirit. They miss the authenticity of what their lips declare. Those who are hypocrites present themselves one way and live another. They may be very religious, but they don't "trust and obey."

So how are we to view these men on the path with Christian? Perhaps they might be termed "brazen hypocrite" and "unregenerate formalist." Neither was genuinely engaged with the holy God who calls us to lives of repentance, obedience, and love.

In contrast, Christian was intent on listening, learning, and responding to the Holy Spirit's leading. He would fail many times, but he had knelt at the cross and committed himself to the long journey to the Celestial City.

He also "refreshed himself" by reading the scroll and drinking at a spring. We can likewise refresh ourselves by reading the Scriptures and enjoying God's presence. The book of James promises, "Come near to God, and he will come near to you."

Paul Tournier, the Swiss psychiatrist who wrote classics such as *The Meaning of Persons*, was asked for his definition of a hypocrite. He answered, "*C'est moi.*" "It is I." Tournier's humility and deep insights permeate his books, and of all people, it's surprising he would call himself a hypocrite. Yet he recognized the truth about the human condition—that we all put on masks and do not always live up to what we preach.

Thank you, Lord, for the richness of your Word and the ways it encourages me and is a light for my path. I don't want to live behind a mask or settle for religious rituals. I long for an authentic faith and close relationship with you. Thank you for the refreshment and spiritual resources you provide. Help me to be an encouragement to others this day, especially to those who are weary.

BEASTS OF THE NIGHT

When Christian reached the top of the hill, two men—Timorous and Mistrust—ran into him at top speed.

"Sirs, what's the matter?" Christian asked them. "You're running the wrong way."

"We are going to the City of Zion," they said, "But the further we go, the more danger we meet; so we are turning back." They described lions on the path ahead and feared they'd be torn to pieces.

Christian was frightened by their words but kept going forward.

As the sun went down, he feared the beasts of the night. Yet, looking up, he saw a palace named Beautiful beside the highway. As he hurried toward it, he came to a narrow passage. There, he saw the lions that had so frightened Timorous and Mistrust.

The porter at the lodge, whose name was Watchful, saw Christian's hesitation and cried out, "Is your strength so small? Do not fear the lions, for they are chained, and are placed there as a trial of faith, and to discover those who have none. Stay in the middle of the path, and no harm shall come to you."

Trembling, Christian heeded the porter's instructions. He heard the lions roar, but they did him no harm.

The famous first line in Scott Peck's book, *The Road Less Traveled*, conveys an obvious truth: "Life is difficult."

For many, that's putting it mildly. We not only experience difficulties, we endure tragic accidents and illnesses. Family dysfunctions crush our spirits. We grieve the inevitable deaths of loved ones. Hymns aptly describe life in our world as "a vale of tears."

When facing his own difficulties, Christian was told, "Stay in the middle of the path, and no harm shall come to you." The lions were chained. It's a promise similar to this one from the Psalms: "Though a thousand fall at your side, though ten thousand are dying around you, these evils will not touch you."

It is a soul-stirring promise, but most of us know that authentic belief does not make us bullet-proof, immune to cancer, or invisible to the beasts of the night. What are we to think about biblical promises such as this, and of the porter's calling out to Christian that the lions were there to test his faith?

The Scriptures emphasize life's brevity, comparing us to mist that disappears, to smoke, or to chaff in the wind. The psalmist states the facts we all live with: "Seventy years are given to us! Some even live to eighty. But even the best years are filled with pain and trouble; soon they disappear and we fly away. . . . Teach us to realize the brevity of life."

What no lion can devour is faith. The writer of Hebrews urges us to "draw near to God with a sincere heart and with the full assurance that faith brings" and to "hold unswervingly to the hope we confess, for he who promised is faithful." Drawing near to God—that is our spiritual protection when the lions roar.

If we are eternal creatures, and those marvelous stanzas of "Amazing Grace" are right—that "when we've been there ten thousand years, bright shining as the sun, we've no less days to sing his praise"—then the crucial dynamics during our brief moments on earth are about loving and obeying God, not ensuring longevity.

That hope gives us considerably less dread of bullets, cancer, and lions. The psalmist declares the life of faith: "So rejoice in the LORD and be glad, all you who obey him! Shout for joy!"

Lord, there are lions roaring in my life right now—dangers and fears that threaten my sense of safety and security. Grant me the faith and courage I need to keep moving forward, trusting that the lions are chained, and that I am safe in your protection and loving care. Give me a heart that is content to trust and rejoice in you.

SHARING HIS STORIES

In the palace named Beautiful, built by the Lord of the hill for the relief and security of pilgrims, Watchful, the porter, introduced Christian to a serious and beautiful young woman named Discretion. She asked where he was from, where he was going, how he got into the way, and what he had seen and met up with.

He told her at length about his fleeing the city and his adventures, and at the last she asked his name.

"It is Christian," he said.

She smiled, but there were tears in her eyes. She then called to three more of the family, Prudence, Piety, and Charity.

"What caused you to take up the pilgrim's life?" asked Piety.

"It was God's doing," Christian said. "I did not know where to go; but as I was trembling and weeping with fear of destruction, a man named Evangelist happened to come to me, and he directed me to the wicket-gate."

When Piety asked if he had been in the house of the Interpreter, he said the memories of what he saw there would stay with him the rest of his life.

"He showed me a stately palace," Christian said, "where the people were clad in gold; and while we were there an adventurous man came and cut his way through the armed men who stood in the door to keep him out, and he was told to come in and win eternal glory. I was overcome with joy and delight at the sight of these things."

The four young women welcomed Christian and shared their mutual faith. Fellowship with other believers is essential for all of us. We benefit from hearing each other's stories. We weep with those who weep, and we rejoice with those who rejoice. Our journeys involve grief and spiritual assaults mixed with occasions of joy.

In his old age, John—Jesus's beloved disciple—wrote this about Christian fellowship: "This one who is life itself was revealed to us. . . . We proclaim to you what we ourselves have actually seen and heard so that you may have fellowship with us. And our fellowship is with the Father and his Son, Jesus Christ. We are writing these things so that you may fully share our joy."

John describes Christian fellowship as an intersection of vital relationships—of God's people with one another and, simultaneously, with the Father and the Son. He writes with amazement at having known and loved the Christ "who is life itself." And in proclaiming to others what he has seen and heard, joy is shared and multiplied.

Yet the joys of fellowship come in the context of spiritual conflict and adversaries. Christian has been confronted by doubters, cowards, and cynics, but he describes with delight the vision Interpreter showed him of a "strong and determined-looking man" fighting his way through armed men to be welcomed into eternal glory.

We, too, are inspired by others who have fought the good fight. We take courage from the beautiful description penned by the writer of Hebrews: "Therefore, since we are surrounded by such a huge crowd of witnesses to the life of faith, let us strip off every weight that slows us down, especially the sin that so easily trips us up. And let us run with endurance the race God has set before us. We do this by keeping our eyes on Jesus, the champion who initiates and perfects our faith."

Lord, you have brought into my life men and women who have loved you and loved others and loved me. Thank you for each of them, and for the many who have nurtured me through their teaching and stories. May I today draw courage and encouragement from their faithfulness, loyalty, and service to others.

PILGRIMS BORN BEGGARS

Christian continued sharing his story with Discretion, Prudence, Piety, and Charity.

"I saw a man hanging, bleeding, upon a tree," he said, "and the very sight of him made my heavy burden fall off my back. . . . I had never seen such a thing before! And while I stood looking up, for then I could not stop looking, three Shining Ones came to me. One of them testified that my sins were forgiven; another stripped me of my rags and gave me this embroidered coat; and the third set the mark that you see on my forehead and gave me this sealed scroll."

Christian went on to tell about the sleeping men with shackles, the two who had come tumbling over the wall, and to share his concern for his family still in the City of Destruction.

Prudence asked about how he now subdued troubling thoughts.

"When I think of what I saw at the cross, that will do it," he replied, "and when I look upon my embroidered coat, that will do it; and when I look into the scroll that I carry, that will do it; and when I think about where I am going, that will do it."

"What is it that makes you so eager to go to Mount Zion?" asked Prudence.

"I hope to see him alive who was hanging dead on the cross," Christian said. "I want to be where I shall die no more, and in the company of those who continually cry, 'Holy, Holy, Holy!'"

When supper was ready, they sat down for a feast. All their talk was of the Lord of the hill who "had stripped himself of his glory" and "made princes of many pilgrims who had been born beggars."

So they talked together until late at night.

Prudence asks a question we might all do well to consider: *How do we subdue troubling thoughts?* As we navigate personal pressures, thorny problems, and relational concerns, how do keep our troublesome thoughts from derailing us? When facing difficulty, how do we nevertheless renew our minds and seek the mind of the Holy Spirit?

Christian remembered the cross, and he looked at the Scriptures in his hand.

Scripture urges us to take our thoughts seriously, and to talk them through with God. "Don't worry about anything," writes the apostle Paul, "instead, pray about everything. Tell God what you need, and thank him for all he has done. . . . Fix your thoughts on what is true, and honorable, and right, and pure, and lovely, and admirable. Think about things that are excellent and worthy of praise." We are not at the mercy of our thoughts—we can choose what we focus on. And when we fix our thoughts on what is true and simultaneously pray (rather than worry) about everything, the Lord helps us to subdue our troubling thoughts.

Christian shows us how to do this in the context of adversity and spiritual warfare. Relevant to Christian's journey and our own is the apostle Paul's declaration, "We are human, but we don't wage war as humans do. We use God's mighty weapons, not worldly weapons, to knock down the strongholds of human reasoning and to destroy false arguments."

With the women of the palace, Christian found that "all their talk . . . was about the Lord." We who find such fellowship are blessed—and fortified for the many challenges of mind and heart we will undoubtedly face on our journey.

Father in heaven, you have made so much that is beautiful and pure and remarkable in our world. Please help me think on these things and your love and care for me rather than all those things that cause me anxiety. And grant me the grace to share your peace with those who feel broken and discouraged.

EQUIPPING PILGRIM FOR BATTLE

Christian slept in a beautiful bedchamber named Peace, and in the morning, the women said he should not leave until they had shown him various rooms in the palace, and how the Lord had performed many mighty acts through his servants.

The women showed him how God's servants had waged valiant fights and wrought righteousness. They gave him a tour of the armory where the Lord had provided shields, helmets, prayers, and shoes that would never wear out.

The next day, his hosts told him they would show him the Delectable Mountains, "which will add to your comfort, for they are nearer your destination than this place." They took him to the top of the house, from which, far in the distance, he saw "a beautiful mountainous country, with woods, vineyards, fruits and flowers of all sorts, springs and fountains, wonderful to behold."

When he asked the name of the country, they said, "It is Immanuel's Land, and it belongs to all pilgrims, as does the hill. And when you get there, you will be able to see the gate of the Celestial City."

Before he left to continue his journey, they returned to the armory. There they equipped him head to foot, in case he was assaulted on the way.

Then the women accompanied him to the foot of the hill, revisiting all the things they had discussed during his stay. "It is hard for a man to go into the Valley of Humiliation, as you are now, and not to slip on the way," Prudence cautioned. "That's why we came out to accompany you down the hill."

The good companions then gave him a loaf of bread, a bottle of wine, and a cluster of raisins to nourish him on his way.

⌒∞⌒

One of the most difficult yet touching times for many of us is when a beloved person or an entire family we've known and loved must move away. We feel the sadness of the parting, the love shared that must now be long-distance, and we see the tears of those gathered 'round to wish godspeed.

In times past, everyone might join hands to sing their farewells:

> *God be with you till we meet again;*
> *When life's perils thick confound you;*
> *Put his arms unfailing round you;*
> *God be with you till we meet again.*

On his departure, Christian was warned, inspired, spiritually equipped, and given practical provisions. Prudence added cautions and expressions of concern.

When we sing "God be with you till we meet again," we not only express our love but our gospel hope. We share our realism about life's thick perils that may assault those we care about. We pray God will put his arms around those we love who will face unforeseen challenges.

Considering what Christian was to face next, it was crucial he be fully equipped.

None of us knows what lies ahead. We all need the support of wise friends, practical provisions, and God's unfailing arms around us.

Lord Jesus, thank you for all those in my life who have shared with me your love and care and provision. Please bless each of them, and help me with those still near to bless and encourage them. Fill me with your Holy Spirit so that I may live with courage, hope, and a willingness to help others.

A DEVILISH CREATURE WITH DARTS

Christian faced great difficulty in the Valley of Humiliation, where he encountered a hideous monster. Apollyon had scales like a fish, wings like a dragon, feet like a bear, a mouth like a lion, and out of his belly came fire and smoke. Christian thought of running away, but he realized he had no armor on his back. So he moved forward.

"Where did you come from and where are you going?" Apollyon demanded to know. Hearing Christian was from the City of Destruction he said, "You are one of my subjects, for all that country is mine, and I am the prince and the god of it. How is it then that you have run away from your king?"

"I have given myself to another, the King of princes," Christian declared.

"I am willing to overlook it if you will turn now and go back," Apollyon said. "You have already been unfaithful to him," he said, and then went on to describe how Christian had fallen into the Slough of Despond, tried to get rid of his burden in wrong ways, lost his scroll, and feared the lions.

"All this is true," Christian admitted, but then added, "I have obtained pardon from my Prince."

Apollyon broke out into a terrible rage. "I am an enemy of the Prince. I hate him and his laws and his people."

"Beware what you do," Christian said, "for I am on the King's highway, the way of holiness."

Apollyon straddled the entire path and said, "I have no fear. Prepare to die." And he threw a flaming dart at the pilgrim's breast.

What are we to make of Apollyon, and how are we to think about evil powers tempting and assaulting us? Does Satan have all the power he claims?

When tempting Jesus, the devil bragged he ruled the kingdoms of the world. "They are mine to give to anyone I please. I will give it all to you if you will worship me." Jesus responded by quoting Scripture, "'You must worship the LORD your God and serve only him.'"

Before his crucifixion, Jesus said, "The time for judging this world has come, when Satan, the ruler of this world, will be cast out."

The ruler of this world? That's startling, and that's scary. We may sing the hymn "This Is My Father's World," for he created it and sent his Son to earth to redeem it. But for now it is tragically fallen. Every day's news reports tell us that.

Christian was told not to stray from the narrow way. He was like a soldier on a path through enemy territory.

We are in our Father's world, but we are vulnerable to the evil powers. In his letter to the church at Ephesus, the apostle Paul describes the devil as "the commander of the powers in the unseen world, . . . the spirit at work in the hearts of those who refuse to obey God." Yet we are given this hope: "God saved you by his grace when you believed."

From Luther's "A Mighty Fortress Is Our God," we can sing, "The Prince of Darkness grim, We tremble not for him; His rage we can endure, For lo! his doom is sure."

Evil comes in many forms. It tempts and assaults each of us in unique ways. We cannot resist Satan's powerful assaults alone. Scripture gives us this battle plan: "So humble yourselves before God. Resist the devil, and he will flee from you. Come close to God, and God will come close to you."

Almighty Father, please grant me your courage and wisdom as I confront evil in its many confusing forms. Help me to be on your side in every battle, and to be an instrument of peace in a world of wars, prisons, and maddening injustices. Thank you for your promise that you will come close to me when I call on you.

HELLISH RAGE

Christian deflected Apollyon's flaming dart with his shield, then drew back. Apollyon rushed, throwing darts thick as hail, wounding Christian in his head, his hand, his foot.

The monster fought back. For more than half a day, Christian manfully resisted, but his wounds made him weaker and weaker.

Apollyon closed in and, wrestling with him, struck him a dreadful blow so he fell hard on the ground. Christian's sword flew from his hand.

"I am sure of you now," the devilish monster said, preparing to strike the last blow.

But Christian caught his sword, saying, "Rejoice not against me, O mine enemy; when I fall I shall arise." With that, he gave Apollyon a deadly thrust.

Then Christian struck again, saying, "Nay, in all these things we are more than conquerors through him that loved us."

Apollyon spread his dragon wings and sped away, and Christian saw him no more for a time. Then he gave thanks, saying, "He with rage that hellish was, did fiercely me engage. But blessed Michael helped me, and I, by dint of sword did make him fly."

Then he received leaves of the tree of life, which healed his wounds. He ate the bread and drank from the bottle that had been given to him earlier, and he was thereby refreshed.

He began his journey once more, his sword drawn, for he said, "Some other enemy may be at hand."

Christian deflected the first flaming dart with his shield, but then the darts kept coming "thick as hail." Though wounded, he kept fighting.

How did he rise from near-defeat and conquer? He relied on the battle plan described by the apostle Paul in Ephesians 6.

Be strong in the Lord and in his mighty power. We can't fight the devil in our own strengths and skills!

Stand firm. A soldier in battle is told exactly that. Despite the monster's terrifying threats, Christian stood his ground.

Put on the belt of truth and the body armor of God's righteousness. The devil finds it hard to penetrate our defenses when we seek God's purity, justice, and mercy.

For shoes, put on the peace that comes from the Good News. To build *esprit de corps*, soldiers shout cadence as they march. When we have God's peace in our hearts—when we walk in harmony with the Holy Spirit—he enables us to resist evil.

Hold up the shield of faith to stop the fiery arrows of the devil. Christian kept believing. Our part is to believe and to pray that God will increase our faith.

Take the sword of the Spirit, which is the Word of God. We, too, can quote scriptures to the devil as Christian did, and as Jesus did when he was tempted in the wilderness.

The Ephesians battle plan includes the chilling context for this fight: "Put on all of God's armor so that you will be able to stand firm against all strategies of the devil. For we are not fighting against flesh-and-blood enemies, but against evil rulers and authorities of the unseen world, against mighty powers in this dark world, and against evil spirits in the heavenly places."

What a picture that gives us of what we are up against! No wonder Paul adds, "Pray in the Spirit at all times and on every occasion. Stay alert and be persistent in your prayers."

Father in heaven, your will be done, on earth as it is in heaven. Bring your will and your power and justice to me and to all your children as we battle against evil and "mighty powers in this dark world." Help me to be wise this day and to put on the armor you provide to gain victory over the enemy.

DRAGONS AND BLASPHEMIES

Christian had to travel through the Valley of the Shadow of Death, for the path to the Celestial City went right through it. At its borders, he met two men who warned, "Back, back!" They had looked in the dark valley and seen hobgoblins, satyrs, and dragons of the pit. They heard a continual howling of people in unspeakable misery.

The two men fled, but Christian drew his sword and continued onward.

The path through the valley was extremely narrow, with a deep ditch on the right, into which many fell and perished. On the left was a marsh with no bottom on which to stand.

Trying to avoid the ditch, Christian almost slipped into the mire of the marsh. He kept going.

Midway through the valley, close to the path, was the mouth of hell. It spewed out flame, smoke, sparks, and hideous noises.

"O Lord, I beg you, deliver my soul!" he cried out.

Sometimes he felt he would be torn to pieces. He heard dreadful noises, and when a company of fiends seemed to come straight at him, he cried out, "I will walk in the strength of the Lord God!"

The demons gave way. But just as he came up to the mouth of the burning pit, one of the wicked ones got behind him. The

75

fiend stepped up softly, and he whispered terrible blasphemies into Christian's ear.

~~~

An attorney once observed, "When I help people make out their wills, I've noticed they always say, '*If* I die.' They never say, '*When* I die.'"

But the *when* is inevitable. The path to the Celestial City goes right through the Valley of the Shadow of Death. The old song reminds us, "You gotta walk that lonesome valley, you gotta walk it by yourself."

Some believers nearing life's end look forward with full confidence to stepping into the arms of a loving God. Others find their faith flickers, and they dread what lies ahead.

We would all like to be among those who feel no fear, seeing death as merely the gateway to a new, joyous life. Pilgrim was not one of them. Here, in this valley, and later in the story, death is a terror to him.

We experience our passages into the next life in very different ways. Anxieties, exuberance, and depression are diverse mixes of biology, experiences, and beliefs. Those who are tormented may take some comfort in identifying with Jesus's struggles in Gethsemane. The author of Hebrews tells us the Lord understands our weaknesses, for he faced the same tests we do. That included dread. In the garden, he was "deeply troubled and distressed," and he told his disciples, "My soul is crushed with grief to the point of death."

Christian feared he would be torn to pieces, but he kept his sword in hand and continued on, no matter what he was feeling. At the mouth of hell, he cried out to the Lord for deliverance. When demons came at him, he fought them back with Scripture.

When we quote Scripture, demons may give way, but they may also keep whispering. Their whispers and our fears may make us dread what's ahead. But God is faithful.

In his letter to the church at Corinth, the apostle Paul assures us we now have every spiritual gift we need, and God will keep us strong to the end: "God will do this, for he is faithful to do what he says, and he has invited you into partnership with his Son, Jesus Christ our Lord."

How strange, Lord, to realize we're all in the Valley of the Shadow of Death. We see others unexpectedly die, and we know we could be next. Help me to rest in your salvation. Comfort me when I must "walk that lonesome valley." And thank you that I don't have to walk it by myself, but I can pray for your loving presence to be with me.

DARKNESS AND DAYBREAK

Christian trudged forward through the Valley of the Shadow of Death. When the demon whispered blasphemies, he was confused and thought the evil words came from his own mind. This was a terrible trial, to think he was blaspheming the Lord he had loved so much.

For a long time, he traveled through the darkness in this disconsolate condition. Then he thought he heard the voice of a man going before him, saying, "Though I walk through the Valley of the Shadow of Death, I will fear no evil, for thou art with me." Then he was glad, for he knew he was not alone in the valley, but others were there who also feared God.

But if God was with them in the darkness, why was God not also with him?

Before long, it was daybreak. Christian, greatly relieved, was buoyed up by his deliverance from all the dangers of his solitary way through the darkness. "He has turned the shadow of death into the morning," Christian declared.

The sun's rising was a mercy, because the second part of the Valley of the Shadow of Death was filled with snares, pits, traps, deep holes, and slopes. As he moved forward, Christian said, "By his light I go through darkness."

Eventually, he came safely to the end of the valley.

In the darkness of the valley, Christian remembered the bold declaration in David's beloved Psalm 23: "Yea, though I walk through the valley of the shadow of death, I will fear no evil: for thou art with me; thy rod and thy staff, they comfort me."

The message of Psalm 23 can be viewed as a summary of God's provisions and engagement throughout life's difficult journey, as experienced in *The Pilgrim's Progress*. Life is full of snares, pits, and traps. Yet the Lord as shepherd lets us rest in green meadows, leads us beside peaceful streams, renews our strength, and guides us along the right paths.

As a young shepherd, David had plenty of enemies and plenty to fear. He addressed God as protector: "I will not be afraid, for you are close beside me. Your rod and your staff protect and comfort me. You prepare a feast for me in the presence of my enemies."

Not only did David view God as the one who gave him a cup overflowing with blessings, he believed God would take the initiative to keep that happening. "Surely your goodness and unfailing love will pursue me all the days of my life, and I will live in the house of the LORD forever."

God pursues us all the days of our lives— that's amazing biblical encouragement!

In very dark moments, Christian found courage and hope in Psalm 23. We, too, can turn to it when we travel through darkness.

Thank you, Lord, for taking the initiative to pursue me with your goodness and unfailing love. Help me to do the same for others who need your peace, especially those who face troubles larger than mine. Guide me, Father, on your path today.

FINDING FAITHFUL

At the top of a hill, Christian could see ahead a man named Faithful. He called out, "Wait, and I will be your companion."

Faithful looked, and Christian called again, "Wait, wait until I catch up with you."

"No," Faithful said, "my life depends on it, for the avenger of blood is behind me." Then Christian used all his strength to catch up.

Faithful, who was also from the City of Destruction, said he had hoped he would have Christian's company on his journey. They discussed meeting Pliable and the Swamp of Despond. Faithful described a flatterer named Wanton who tried to seduce him, promising all kinds of carnal satisfaction.

"Thank God you have escaped her," Christian said.

"I don't know whether I completely escaped her or not," Faithful admitted.

"Why, I trust you did not consent to her desires?"

"No, not to defile myself; for I remembered an old writing I had seen, which said, 'Her steps lead straight to hell.' So I shut my eyes, so I would not be bewitched by her looks. Then she spoke harshly to me, and I went my way."

The "old writing" Faithful remembered seeing was Proverbs—and not just a verse or two about the consequences of adultery, but a lengthy story with dramatic images and severe warnings. Proverbs' message for us today—considering all the stories of broken and bitter lives splashed on supermarket tabloids—is more relevant than ever, but also unheeded. If an effective video were made of Proverbs 6 and 7—which detail lessons for daily life and warnings about immoral women—it just might go viral. Would it jolt viewers?

Sadly, many today are likely too jaded to be jolted by anything. In a culture where marriage is routinely tossed aside and paternity tests are required to identify fathers, there is no adultery or fornication— just people being "sexually active." The "open-marriage" movements and hostility to biblical values have been disastrous, not only for women and men, but especially for children.

Proverbs, a book of wisdom, doesn't pull any punches about the consequences of such illicit behavior: "Can a man scoop a flame into his lap and not have his clothes catch on fire? Can he walk on hot coals and not blister his feet? So it is with the man who sleeps with another man's wife. . . . The man who commits adultery is an utter fool, for he destroys himself."

Faithful didn't let Wanton seduce him, but he admitted he hadn't fully escaped her wiles. We are all sexual beings, and we all must deal with our biology. In our sex-saturated world, we constantly face temptations.

God created us, and he created something beautiful when he created sex. Scripture celebrates it, even explicitly in Song of Solomon. And from Proverbs we read, "Let your wife be a fountain of blessing for you. . . . Let her breasts satisfy you always. May you always be captivated by her love."

Heavenly Father, I have all sorts of desires today, for food and comfort and all the physical drives of being human. Guide me, Lord, in how to serve you, enjoy you, and to walk in your presence with a pure heart. Thank you for your grace and guidance. Help me to listen for your Spirit's voice.

THREE DAUGHTERS

As they walked, Faithful told Christian about an aged man named First Adam who lived in the town of Deceit. He had offered Faithful many delights, and promised to make Faithful his heir if he'd come to work for him. Not only that, he could marry all three of his daughters: The Lust of the Flesh, The Lust of the Eyes, and The Pride of Life.

Faithful had been inclined to accept the aged man's offer, until he saw these words written on his forehead, "Put off the old man and his deeds."

"And what then?" Christian asked.

"It came burning hot into my mind," said Faithful, "that whatever he said and however he flattered, when he got me home to his house, he would sell me as a slave."

When Faithful tried to leave, the old man reviled him, grabbed him, and gave him a deadly jerk backward that made him cry out, "O wretched man!'

After that, when Faithful had been halfway up the hill called Difficulty, a man came after him swift as the wind, overtook him, and knocked him down. When Faithful asked why, the man said, "Because of your secret interest in the First Adam." Then he beat him until Faithful cried, "Have mercy!" But the man didn't know how to show mercy, and he knocked him down again.

Faithful said to Christian, "No doubt he would have killed me if someone had not told him to stop."

Christian identified the man who beat him as Moses, who spares no one who breaks his law.

Faithful said the man who told Moses to stop was the Lord, for he saw the holes in his hands and his side.

Why do we need mercy?

Why do we need grace?

And why do so many tear up as they sing "Amazing Grace"?

When we try to live well without God, our true conditions are revealed by our failures as we're halfway up the hill. We get beaten up by the law of Moses. But when we call out to Christ, he intercedes for us and brings us mercy and grace.

The apostle Peter captures the magnificence of mercy and grace, and his words are well worth reading and absorbing: "All praise to God, the Father of our Lord Jesus Christ. It is by his great mercy that we have been born again, because God raised Jesus Christ from the dead. Now we live by great expectation, and we have a priceless inheritance—an inheritance that is kept in heaven for you, pure and undefiled, beyond the reach of change and decay. . . . So be truly glad. There is wonderful joy ahead, even though you must endure many trials for a little while."

The pages of *The Pilgrim's Progress* are filled with many trials, and in our own ways we may well face them all. We need cleansing, courage, guidance, and grace from God as we endure our troubles day after day.

Peter goes on to encourage his readers with these words: "You love him even though you have never seen him. Though you do not see him now, you trust him, and you rejoice with a glorious, inexpressible joy. The reward from trusting him will be the salvation of your souls."

Thank you, Lord, for your grace. Help me today to trust and obey as I navigate all the issues and challenges that come my way. I give you praise for your wonderful works and ask that my actions and my life will honor you and bless others.

SHAME:
THE VILLAIN

Faithful told Christian he had met a bold villain named Shame who objected to religion, saying it was a pitiful, low, sneaking business. He considered a tender conscience unmanly, and said that few mighty, rich, or wise people cared about religion. It was a shame to sit mourning under a sermon. It was a shame to ask a neighbor's forgiveness for petty faults. Religion made a man seem odd to great people because of its objection to a few vices.

"And what did you say to him?" Christian asked.

"Say! I didn't know what to say at first," Faithful admitted. "He kept at me so that my face became red."

But then Faithful remembered something about the day of judgment. "We shall not be awarded death or life according to the bullying spirits of this world," he said, "but according to the wisdom and law of the Highest . . . what God says is best, though all the men in the world are against it. . . . The poor man who loves Christ is richer than the greatest man in the world who hates him."

Remembering these realities had enabled Faithful to say, "Shame, depart! You are an enemy to my salvation. If I am ashamed of his ways and servants now, how can I expect his blessing?"

Yet Shame had continued to follow him, whispering in his ear about things wrong with religion. Finally, Faithful had gotten past him.

"We must resist Shame," Christian said. He quoted Solomon: "The wise shall inherit glory, but shame shall be the promotion of fools."

As secularism grows more and more powerful and threatens to marginalize Christian values, this episode in the pilgrim's story is particularly relevant. The shaming of believers has become common.

Sometimes Christians have said or done foolish things deserving censure. We must be sensitive to historic faults and atrocities committed in the name of religion, including our own. At the same time, core beliefs now increasingly clash, and media sensationalize the differences. Christians' concerns are often caricatured as old-school, unhealthy, and even absurd.

As believers, we walk a fine line. We are all about grace and God's love, not about condemning others. Yet we routinely see devastations that come from discarding God's Word and his redemptive, transforming power.

How do we walk that line in an increasingly polarized world? We have Paul's example of courage and wisdom. "I am not ashamed of this Good News about Christ," he wrote. "It is the power of God at work." Paul hoped and fully expected he would never be ashamed, but that his life would bring honor to Christ.

That's where walking the line starts—with authenticity in our personal lives.

The psalmist affirms that none who keep God's decrees have reason to fear shame: "I will speak to kings about your laws, and I will not be ashamed."

Whether we are speaking out, or simply obeying the greatest commandments—to love God and love others—we need great humility. Most of all, we need the guidance and presence of the Holy Spirit.

Lord, help me to discern what I must stand for or against. When I feel shame, grant me courage and a sense of your grace and peace. Help me to endure refining fires by your grace and wisdom. Increase my genuine concern for others.

"A DEVIL AT HOME"

As Faithful and Christian continued their journey, Faithful noticed a fellow pilgrim named Talkative and invited him to join them.

Talkative impressed Faithful with his affirmations of the need for repentance, grace, prayer, and the consolations of the gospel.

"What a brave companion we have!" said Faithful to Christian. "Surely this man will make an excellent pilgrim."

"Despite his fine tongue, he is a contemptible fellow," Christian said, for he knew the man.

Faithful was startled, but Christian said, "I will tell you more about him. This man enjoys any company and any talk. . . . Religion has no place in his heart, or his home, or his behavior; he is all talk, and his religion is his tongue."

"Then I have been greatly deceived by this man," Faithful admitted.

"You may be sure of it," said Christian. "I have been with his family. . . . His house is as empty of religion as the white of an egg is of flavor. There is neither prayer there, nor sign of repentance for sin. . . . He gives religion a bad name. The folks who know him say, 'He's a saint abroad and a devil at home.' Certainly his poor family finds it so; he is rude and abusive."

As they continued walking, Christian added, "The soul of religion is the practical part: 'Pure religion and undefiled, before God and the Father, is this, to visit the fatherless and widows in their affliction, and to keep himself unspotted from the world.' This, Talkative is not aware of. He thinks that hearing and saying will make a good Christian, and thus he deceives his own soul."

⸎

Christian's description of the soul of religion as "the practical part" resonates with those of us who seek authenticity in our faith. We recognize our mandate to care for the afflicted. We struggle to keep unspotted by the world and to avoid hypocrisy. We take seriously the admonition of the prophet Micah: "The Lord has told you what is good, and this is what he requires of you: to do what is right, to love mercy, and to walk humbly with your God."

Yet what are we to think about Faithful's gullibility? He is unaware he's giving a pass to someone who abuses his family and fakes his spiritual life. Is there something here we should take to heart?

Unfortunately, Talkative—the saint abroad and devil at home—severely violates his conscience with hypocrisy. His duplicity devastates his family and, as Christian points out, gives religion a bad name. Sometimes his hypocrisy is obvious; sometimes it isn't, which is perhaps why Faithful failed to recognize it.

Scripture tells us to love God with our minds, to ask him for wisdom, and to test the spirits. Faithful, with more awareness, may have picked up on his new friend's hypocrisy. Since he did not, it was good that Christian was there to warn him.

Church discipline and discerning hypocrisy as separate from other human frailties, such as dysfunctional patterns or mental illness, are subjects for thick books and require great sensitivity and wisdom. There are no easy answers! Yet we are called to be instruments of God's peace, even in the midst of such troubling situations.

Jesus said to his disciples, "I am sending you out as sheep among wolves. So be as shrewd as snakes and harmless as doves."

Father in heaven, keep me from talking one way and living another. Let me be a blessing to others instead of causing them resentment and pain. And, I pray, give me both wisdom and courage when I learn of situations needing a loving, thoughtful word . . . or more.

VANITY FAIR

Evangelist caught up with Christian and Faithful and greeted them: "Peace be with you, dearly beloved." He warned them they must pass through many tribulations to enter the kingdom of heaven. He gave them this parting encouragement: "Behave like men and commit yourselves to your faithful Creator and continue to do good."

When Faithful and Christian emerged from the wilderness, they saw a town ahead named Vanity. It had a fair named Vanity Fair at which were sold all sorts of vain things: "houses, lands, trades, places, honors, promotions, titles, lusts, pleasures, and delights of all sorts . . . where one could always see jugglers, cheats, games, plays, fools, mimics, tricksters, and scoundrels of every kind."

The path to the Celestial City passed right through this town. The Blessed Prince was long ago tempted in this town by the devil, who showed him all the kingdoms of this world, but the Prince did not spend one cent on the vanities offered him.

As Christian and Faithful entered the fair, the town was soon in an uproar around them. The townspeople viewed the pilgrims as madmen with strange speech who refused to buy their wares. The fair's governor was called, and he deputized friends to take the two men into custody.

Christian and Faithful explained they were pilgrims and strangers in the world, and they were going to the heavenly Jerusalem. But the deputies beat them, smeared them with mud, and put them into a cage to make a spectacle of them.

Many of the townspeople laughed and made sport of them, but a few saw they were sober men who meant no one harm. When the people began fighting among themselves, Christian and Faithful were blamed for causing trouble.

To set an example for others, Christian and Faithful were mercilessly beaten, paraded through the fair in chains, then put back in the cage.

Remembering that Evangelist had told them such things would happen, the two pilgrims comforted each other and committed themselves to the will of God.

We all need food, clothing, shelter. So when do necessities become the wares of Vanity Fair? When do good things of life—art, music, beautiful clothing, fine food—become snares? And how do we live as pilgrims in an affluent society and not become like the townsmen of Vanity Fair?

We see the contrast in the apostle Paul's instructions to his protégé, Timothy. "True godliness with contentment is itself great wealth," he writes. "So if we have enough food and clothing, let us be content. But people who long to be rich fall into temptation and are trapped by many foolish and harmful desires that plunge them into ruin and destruction."

That's an apt description of Vanity Fair's customers—trapped by their desires and plunged into ruin. They live without wonder and gratitude for all the gifts of life that come from the Father. Disconnected from God, they vent their anger on those who love him.

Paul goes on to issue a warning that applies to both rich and poor: "For the love of money is the root of all kinds of evil." And he gives his apprentice these instructions: "But you, Timothy, are a man of God; so run from all these evil things. Pursue righteousness and a godly life, along with faith, love, perseverance, and gentleness. Fight the good fight for the true faith. Hold tightly to the eternal life to which God has called you."

The world does not always appreciate such faithfulness. The way Christian and Faithful were tormented made no sense at all, as some in the town observed. But when events seem absurd, God's Word instructs and is as precious as gold.

Paul continues with this advice to Timothy: "Teach those who are rich in this world not to be proud and not to trust in their money. Their trust should be in God, who richly gives us all we need for our enjoyment."

If the love of money leads to all kinds of evil, loving the Lord our God with heart, mind, and soul leads to life eternal with him—whatever our present troubles.

◦◦◦

Lord, issues related to money and materialism are often hard for me to figure out. Please help me, I pray, to have a love for beauty and craftsmanship, yet a simplicity of heart and a love for others that far exceeds my desire for earthly things. Give me a generous spirit and an attitude formed by your work in me.

A VERDICT
OF GUILTY

Christian and Faithful were brought before a Vanity Fair judge named Lord Hate-good. Three witnesses testified—Envy, Superstition, and Pickthank.

Envy said Christian and Faithful were vile men, not respecting Vanity Fair's laws and customs. Superstition said they were troublemakers who had accused the town of worshiping in vain. Pickthank accused them of speaking contemptuously of the Lord Carnal Delight, the Lord Luxurious, the Lord Desire of Vain-glory, and of old Lord Lechery.

Judge Hate-good declared Faithful a renegade and traitor and said he deserved to die.

Faithful was allowed to speak in his own defense. "I never said anything but this: That any rule, or laws, or custom, or people that are against the Word of God are diametrically opposed to Christianity. . . . A divine faith is required in the worship of God; but there can be no divine faith without a divine revelation of the will of God."

The judge gave instructions to the jury, including Mr. Malice, Mr. Love-lust, Mr. Liar, and Mr. Cruelty. Following their deliberations, the foreman declared, "I see clearly that this man is a heretic." The jury delivered a verdict of guilty and a sentence of death.

They scourged and buffeted Faithful, stoned him, pricked him with swords, and burned him to ashes at the stake.

As this was happening, a heavenly chariot and horses were waiting. As soon as Faithful had been killed, he was taken up into the chariot. It carried him through the clouds, with sounds of trumpets, on the nearest way to the Celestial Gate.

Christian was returned to prison. Later, he escaped, and as he journeyed on, he sang:

> *Sing, Faithful, sing, and let thy name survive;*
> *For though they killed thee, thou are yet alive.*

When we read accounts of martyrdoms, questions arise. *Why Faithful and not Christian? Why are people in distant countries killed for their faith and not me? Could it happen where I live? How would I act if they came for me?* In a sense, these are the same questions we might ask about cancer and accidents and war.

The Bible goes to the heart of all our questions and is full of bracing encouragements. Jesus said to person after person, "Fear not." Paul wrote Timothy, "God has not given us a spirit of fear, but of power and of love and of a sound mind."

We need all that and more to navigate the dangers and trials of our fallen world.

Fallen indeed! Although Vanity Fair is a literary device set in another century and its characters are odd, to say the least, they're not unknown to us. Lord Hate-good. Mr. Liar. Old Lord Lechery. The names are descriptive of what we know only too well.

In this age of digital media, with its barrage of disturbing videos and reports, we routinely see personalities embodying Bunyan's characters. In fact, if someone were to create a board game with the names, it wouldn't be difficult to identify match-ups.

Lord Hate-good could be one of those comedians who cleverly ridicule "do-gooders" and the chaste.

Mr. Liar? Several prominent names fit him only too well.

How about old Lord Lechery? Anyone come to mind who's made multimillions from the lecherous use of women's bodies?

In our towns and on our screens, we see a great mixture of people. Some are like the townspeople of Vanity Fair; fortunately, others contribute to life with empathy and integrity. Scripture and *The Pilgrim's Progress* sharpen our capacity to discern.

We are called to be among those who courageously live by the Spirit, through life or death, on the path to the Celestial City.

Lord Jesus, when I hear of innocent people tortured and of hatred against what's good, I recall that you were innocent and good when you were crucified. In the midst of this world's mortal troubles, I pray you will give me courage and a sense of your presence. Grant me faith to believe that whatever happens, the best is yet to come.

SILVER-SLIPPER RELIGION

Christian did not go on alone. Joining him was Hopeful, who at the fair had been won to the Lord by the words and behavior of Christian and Faithful.

The two of them soon overtook a man named By-ends from the town of Fair-speech, who said he was going to the Celestial City. He told them he and his wife, who was Lady Feigning's daughter, differed in religion from those of the stricter sort in only two small points: "First, we never go against the wind and the tide; and second, we are always most zealous when religion walks in silver slippers and when the sun shines and when the people applaud what we believe."

"If you want to go with us," Christian said, "you must go against wind and tide. . . . You must also own religion when it is in rags, as well as when it is in silver slippers, and stand by it when it is bound in irons, as well as when it is applauded in the streets."

"You must not impose your beliefs on me," By-ends responded. "Leave me my freedom, and let me go with you."

But they parted ways. Later, By-ends joined other companions who viewed Christian and Hopeful as overly righteous and rigid, judging and condemning everyone but themselves. By-ends and his companions emphasized enjoying God's provisions and, if necessary, changing one's principles to keep them. One reasoned that, by becoming religious, a man might increase his business prospects and get a rich wife. "Therefore," he said, "to become religious to get all these is a good and profitable plan."

But when By-ends and his companions shared these ideas, Christian responded, "Even a babe in religion may answer ten thousand such questions. For if it is unlawful to follow Christ for loaves, as it is, how much more abominable is it to make him and religion a stalking-horse to promote themselves or their business."

Christian then gave examples from the Scriptures. On hearing Christian's response, the men were sobered, silenced, and lagged behind.

The benefits of true religion are not only the delights of heaven to come. On earth, we increase the odds for a happy and meaningful life when we express constant gratitude to God, love and care for others, and avoid vices that destroy the body. We are created to enjoy such benefits, even as we proceed in our pilgrimage through "dangers, toils, and snares."

Yet we sometimes still take God's benefits for granted, and slide into silver-slipper thinking. When others view our beliefs with disdain, how willing might we be to adjust or soft-pedal our beliefs and commitments to ingratiate ourselves or avoid offending?

This episode in the pilgrim's story is not only a warning to avoid putting religion on and off as if it were a disposable uniform. It is also a call to think deeply, to evaluate our beliefs, and to pray fervently for the Holy Spirit's affirmations on our beliefs and how we act on them. The last thing we want to do is fight for beliefs and attitudes that may seem right but have none of the Spirit of Christ.

It's helpful to be reminded of what Jesus identified as the first and greatest commandment: "You must love the LORD your God with all your heart, all your soul, and all your mind." We must engage in our pilgrimage with all our faculties as we encounter new questions, urgencies, and challenges to what we have come to believe.

The Apostle Paul tells us, "all creation has been groaning as in the pains of childbirth right up to the present time. And we believers also groan, even though we have the Holy Spirit within us as a foretaste of future glory." Paul goes on to say we wait with eager hope for our new bodies. Our bodies now may be filled with the Holy Spirit, but they are not yet glorified. Even so, when we are weak and don't know what to pray for, "the Holy Spirit pleads for us."

The book of James, always practical, counsels, "If you need wisdom, ask our generous God, and he will give it to you. He will not rebuke you for asking."

Lord, I confess that part of my motivation for following your path is to receive your benefits, both here and in heaven. Help me to know when that brings you a smile, and when I am more interested in your blessings than in you. Cleanse me, I pray, and draw me into your presence.

THE HILL CALLED LUCRE

Christian and Hopeful came to Hill Lucre, so called because it had a silver mine. Some travelers passing by turned aside to see it because it was a rarity. But when they got too close to the edge of the pit, the ground gave way under them, and they were killed.

A little off the road, a man named Demas called politely, "Hello there! Come over here and I will show you something."

"What would be worthwhile enough to make us leave the way?" asked Christian.

"There is a silver mine here, and some are digging in it for treasure. If you will come, with very little effort you may richly provide for yourselves."

"Let us go see," said Hopeful.

"Not I," said Christian. "I have heard of this place before, and how many have been killed here; and besides that, treasure is a trap to those who seek it. . . . Let us not move a step toward it, but keep on our way."

Demas again invited them to come see, but Christian rebuked him. "If we turn aside at all, our Lord the King will certainly hear of it and will put us to shame, and we desire to stand with boldness before him."

Demas cried out that he was one of their brothers, and if they would wait a little while, he would walk with them.

But Christian and Hopeful kept moving.

Not far behind them on the path were By-ends and his companions, who readily responded to Demas's invitation. Whether they fell into the pit, went down to dig, or were smothered by poisonous gases was unknown, but they were never again seen in the way.

The apostle Paul acknowledges a man named Demas in his epistles. In Philemon, Paul describes him as a coworker. In Colossians, Paul writes, "Luke, the beloved doctor, sends his greetings, and so does Demas." So far, it appears as if the man is a believer in good standing. But then Paul writes this, "Demas has deserted me because he loves the things of this life."

That's all we know about Demas, but centuries later, we know his spiritual heirs—Christians who are lured off the path by their love of earthly treasure.

But what, we may ask, is wrong with "loving the things of this life"? Shouldn't we enjoy God's good creation of food and clothing, art and music, museums and travel? Aren't we to praise God for his creation and "be glad in it"?

Yes, we're invited to enjoy and appreciate, but not to forget who made *everything*. When we continually remind ourselves to love the Lord with heart, mind, and soul—to love him more than all else—we enhance all we enjoy.

When we see a spectacular sunrise or magnificent scenery, sharing the experience with a companion enhances our enjoyment. When God is our companion, when we practice his presence and stay on his path, we enhance our enjoyment of his creation. And staying on his path means we don't love our treasures more than God, or love them more than our neighbor.

"You make known to me the path of life," declares the psalmist, "in your presence there is fullness of joy." We can focus our thoughts on God's wonders and love. The psalms repeatedly promise we will find "delight" in walking the path of his commands.

Even so, we need more than self-effort. Through hard experience, we learn our steadiness and growth come when we call on the Lord. We need God's guidance and strength, and we need to ask him for both. We find this promise in Psalm 32: "The LORD says, 'I will guide you along the best pathway for your life. I will advise you and watch over you.'"

There's a bit of Demas in all of us. That's why we might also ponder these words penned by the prophet Jeremiah: "This is what the LORD says: 'Stop at the crossroads and look around. Ask for the old, godly way, and walk in it. Travel its path, and you will find rest for your souls.'"

Heavenly Father, left to my own devices, my thoughts can dwell too long on the treasures of this world—what I want and what I think I need. Please help me to choose your ways and to seek your wisdom. Show me how I can bless and encourage others, and thank you for your many blessings to me.

TWO MEADOWS

The pilgrims' path went along the bank of a pleasant river, where they walked with delight. They drank the water, which enlivened their weary spirits. They ate the fruit from trees and enjoyed a meadow filled with beautiful lilies, where they slept and could rest safely. They stayed in that place several days and sang of its fragrance and comforts.

As they continued their journey, the path and river soon parted, and the path turned rough. It was hard on their feet and greatly discouraging them.

Then they saw it—a set of steps leading into By-path Meadow. "If this meadow lies alongside our pathway, let's go over into it," Christian said. Climbing the steps, he looked across and saw a path running along the other side of the fence. It looked like much easier going.

"Come, good Hopeful," he called out, "let's go over."

"But what if this path should lead us out of the way?" Hopeful asked.

"That's not likely," Christian replied. "Look, doesn't it go parallel to the pathway?"

The new path was easy on their feet. They saw walking not far ahead a man named Vain-confidence. When he told them he, too, was heading for the Celestial Gate, Christian said to Hopeful, "Look, didn't I tell you so? See, we are right."

All seemed well. But then night came and it grew very dark.

Vain-confidence, who was walking ahead of them, suddenly fell into a deep pit. They called out to him, but there was no answer. He had been dashed to pieces.

It began to rain hard. The pathway flooded. Dreadful thunder and lightning threatened.

"Oh, I wish I had kept on my way!" Hopeful groaned.

Christian said he was greatly sorry for leading him out of the way. Hopeful said he forgave him.

Then they heard a voice saying, "Let thine heart be towards the highway, even the way that thou wentest, turn again." But the waters had risen, making the pathway back very dangerous. Over and over they attempted to go back in the darkness, but they were exhausted and nearly drowned.

Not far from them was Doubting Castle, owned by Giant Despair.

Many of us have been fortunate enough to experience pleasant meadows in our lives. We've had times when we felt safe, had meaningful work or educational experiences, enjoyed friends and family who loved us, and we felt spiritually nourished.

Yet all of us come to rough patches, as Christian and Hopeful did. Toxic workplaces and job losses, family dysfunctions, serious illnesses and accidents, church splits. We get blindsided by rough reversals. We might even find ourselves immobilized like the proverbial deer in headlights—disoriented by what's happening, plagued by spiritual doubts, and vulnerable to unwise decisions.

In that condition, we might see someone like Vain-confidence walking along without a care in the world. Plenty of people seem to be navigating life just fine, confident that their path is as good as that of an authentic pilgrim. Their confidence can make us wonder if a life of obedience and sacrifice and loving God with heart, mind, and soul is necessary.

Oswald Chambers observed that many things are perfectly legitimate, "but if you are going to concentrate on God you cannot do them. . . . The unspiritual person says, 'Whatever is wrong with that? How absurd you are!'"

Unfortunately for Christian and Hopeful, there were severe consequences for easing onto a less demanding path and justifying their choice because someone else had done the same. Scripture tells us, "There is a path before each person that seems right, but it ends in death."

Sometimes we must carefully judge and pray earnestly about what looks like a pleasant meadow just a bit off the path. And, unlike Christian, who dismissed Hopeful's concerns, we may need to listen carefully to the cautions of other Christians.

Heavenly Father, you know so well the temptations I struggle against and the ones that could blindside me. Take up the battle for me. May your Holy Spirit warn me and guide me, creating in me the desire and the power to embrace your will and to walk your pathway.

GIANT DESPAIR

When Giant Despair caught Christian and Hopeful on his property, he prodded them into a dark, nasty dungeon inside his castle, and left them for days without bread, water, or light.

When the giant asked his wife, Diffidence, what he should do with the prisoners, she advised, "Beat them without mercy in the morning."

So, Giant Despair got a heavy club, went down into the dungeon, scolded the prisoners as if they were dogs, beat them so badly they couldn't move, and then left them in their misery.

The next night, learning the prisoners were still alive, Diffidence suggested Giant Despair counsel them to kill themselves. In the morning, seeing their condition from the beating, he told them their only way to escape was to do away with themselves—with knife, rope, or poison. "Why should you choose life," he asked, "when it is filled with so much bitterness?"

"Brother, what shall we do?" Christian asked Hopeful. "The grave looks better to me than this dungeon. Shall we take the giant's advice?"

Hopeful responded that doing so would be against their Lord's commands, and that others had escaped the hand of Giant Despair. "I am resolved to take heart and try my utmost to get away from him. . . . Let's be patient and endure for a while longer. In time we may escape."

When the giant returned and found his prisoners still alive, he fell into a terrible rage. He declared they would soon wish they had never been born.

They trembled greatly, but Hopeful reminded Christian of his bravery battling Apollyon and of the terrors he had overcome.

"Remember how brave you were at Vanity Fair," said Hopeful, "neither afraid of the chain, nor the cage, nor even bloody death."

Christian and Hopeful made themselves vulnerable to Giant Despair by wandering off the path. Despair can occur that way, and the pilgrims' foolishness has lessons for us. Yet we know that Giant Despair sometimes also bludgeons those whose feet have not strayed from God's path.

When life turns dark and bleak, when we despair of life itself, sunny spiritual talk doesn't register. When we or those we love are trapped in a dark dungeon, we may be mystified and feel helpless.

Much has been written about the dark night of the soul, including accounts of despair that ultimately deepen believers' faith. And much has also been written about severe depression, its causes, and suggested therapies. We are fortunate so many resources are available to us, both spiritual and medical. But when Giant Despair chains someone in his dungeon, the dark night may last a long time.

Christian, so broken he was ready to take the giant's advice to commit suicide, fortunately listened to the good counsel of Hopeful. This faithful companion was true to his name, despite the bleakness of their circumstances.

In our broken world, we all need hope, and we need the encouragement and prayers of others. The apostle Paul writes that we have been called to "one glorious hope for the future." And he models how we as pilgrims can pray and care for one another: "As we pray to our God and Father about you, we think of your faithful work, your loving deeds, and the enduring hope you have because of our Lord Jesus Christ."

Enduring hope. When trapped in a dungeon of despair, hope doesn't always feel all that enduring. But as believers, we can persist in praying for one another, and in pursuing faith, hope, and love.

Lord Jesus, help me to cling to the hope that transcends my circumstances. Fill me with the hope that comes from your Holy Spirit. Through all my troubles, help me to listen for your wisdom, to rely on your power, and to never give up.

THE KEY
CALLED PROMISE

Night came again, and Mrs. Diffidence and Giant Despair were in bed. When she asked about the prisoners, the giant replied, "They are rugged scoundrels."

"Take them into the castle yard," she advised, "and show them the bones and skulls of those you have already killed, and make them believe that before the week is out you will also tear them in pieces, as you have done to those before them."

In the morning, Giant Despair took Christian and Hopeful to the castle yard and showed them the bones. "These once were pilgrims as you are," he said. "I tore them in pieces; and so I will do to you within ten days." With that, he beat them all the way back to the dungeon.

About midnight the pilgrims began to pray. They continued in earnest prayer almost until daybreak.

Then Christian broke out in a passionate speech. "What a fool I am to lie in a stinking dungeon when I can freely walk away! I have a key in my bosom called Promise, that will, I am persuaded, open any lock in Doubting Castle."

He pulled out the key of Promise, and as he turned it in the dungeon door, the bolt slid back and the door flew open. When the pair got to the outer door leading to the castle yard, it opened, too.

Then they went to the iron gate. Though it was very hard to turn, the key did open it. They threw the gate open to make their escape.

Roused by the creaking noise of the gate, Giant Despair rose hastily to pursue his prisoners. But his legs failed, and he could not go after them.

When the pilgrims had gone over the fence where they had originally crossed, they erected a pillar to warn others from crossing there. They engraved on it these words: "Over these steps is the way to Doubting Castle, which is kept by Giant Despair, who despises the King of the Celestial Country and seeks to destroy his holy pilgrims."

Much like Christian and Hopeful in the giant's dungeon, the author of Lamentations is a soul in despair. Crushed by horrific violence done to his people, he laments that he has been led into a dark place. He is walled in, bound in heavy chains, and he cannot escape. "Everything I had hoped for from the LORD is lost!" he cries out. "The thought of my suffering . . . is bitter beyond words."

No wonder he feels buried in a dark place! Of his friends and loved ones he writes, "See them lying in the streets—young and old, boys and girls, killed by the swords of the enemy. . . . No one has escaped or survived. The enemy has killed all the children whom I carried and raised." His lament is poignant and deep.

Although Lamentations was written thousands of years ago, we can empathize and relate to the writer's sorrow. In the news, we've seen similar horrors inflicted on innocent men, women, and children. How does anyone deal with the slaughter of other human beings, and especially of people one knows and loves?

In spite of what he has witnessed and suffered, the grieving man writes this profound assertion of faith, "I will never forget this awful time. . . . Yet I still dare to hope when I remember this: The faithful love of the LORD never ends! His mercies never cease. Great is his faithfulness; his mercies begin afresh each morning."

Great is his faithfulness. Many of us have sung those words and quoted that his mercies begin afresh each morning, but perhaps few of us have sung them in the midst of such devastation as the writer of Lamentations endured.

We can take heart from the fact that the Bible is realistic about life's harsh realities. Yet it also reveals how even our sufferings are mysteriously interwoven with God's mercies and promises. Christian's journey mirrors that truth. It is a story that relentlessly depicts evil and the demonic powers, but also demonstrates the deeper and abiding power of God's promises.

Christian's Promise key freed him from despair. "Your promises have been thoroughly tested," writes the psalmist, "that is why I love them so much."

The apostle Peter writes, "By his divine power, God has given us everything we need for living a godly life. . . . And because of his glory and excellence, he has given us great and precious promises. These are the promises that enable you to share his divine nature and escape the world's corruption."

Lord, fill me with your Spirit of peace when I experience calamity or when I fear what is about to happen. Grant me the courage to rely on the promise that your mercies are new every morning, especially when I am anxious and without peace.

SEEING THE CELESTIAL CITY

Christian and Hopeful came to the Delectable Mountains, with gardens, orchards, vineyards, and fountains. They drank and washed themselves and ate freely from the vineyards.

On the tops of the mountains, near the pathway, shepherds tended their flocks. The two pilgrims approached the shepherds and asked, "Who do these Delectable Mountains belong to?"

"The mountains are Immanuel's Land," a shepherd responded.

"Is this the way to the Celestial City?" Christian asked.

"You are just on the path," the shepherd said.

"How far is it?" Christian asked.

"Too far for any but those who really want to get there," the shepherd said.

After hearing the pilgrims' stories, the shepherds invited Christian and Hopeful to stay for a while. They showed them pleasant wonders and warned them of deadly dangers, including the roads to hell they must avoid.

"We had better cry to the Strong for strength," the pilgrims said to each other.

"Yes," said the shepherds, "and you will need to use it when you have it too."

The shepherds also let them look through their telescope to see the gates of the Celestial City in the distance. When the pilgrims were about to depart, one shepherd gave them a map of the way.

Another warned them to beware of the Flatterer.

A third told them not to sleep on the Enchanted Ground.

The fourth bid them Godspeed.

From imprisonment in the castle of Giant Despair to a warm welcome by shepherds in Delectable Mountains, the pilgrims' journey includes stark contrasts. Many of us experience similar contrasts in our own lives. Grief and loss come to all, yet God is faithful.

Just as the pilgrims were attentive to the shepherds' warnings about the last leg of their journey, we need to seek out and be attentive to wisdom. The rapid changes of a globalized world often leave us feeling vulnerable and in need of great courage and faith. When so much is changing so fast, we know we can be caught unawares. What might we learn from the wisdom of the shepherds?

They focused the pilgrims' gaze on the future by giving them a look at the Celestial City. We need to be reminded that this world is not all there is. When we pray to our Father, "Thy will be done, on earth as it is in heaven," we affirm that the activities of heaven are far different from what is going on here, and that we have spiritual battles to fight.

In her book *Heaven*, Joni Eareckson Tada writes, "What's odd is, the closer I draw to Jesus, the more intense the heat of the battle. Never do I feel more on the frontline of this battle than when I offer praise to God. Right in the middle of adoring him in prayer or singing a praise hymn, my heart will go wandering off into some wicked thought. I have to grab my heart by the aorta and jerk it in line time and again!"

Joni writes with realism about our short time on earth, and with awe about the anticipation of heaven. She understands the stark contrasts so many of us experience in the life of faith.

The shepherds provided Christian and Hopeful with a map of the way, and we have our own map in the Scriptures.

When the pilgrims heard of deadly dangers ahead and said they'd better "cry to the Strong for strength," it's instructive that the shepherds affirmed both the need to call for God's strength and then to use it. How God strengthens us in our weakness, and how we must then act on it, is a mystery theologians love to discuss and debate. The shepherds simply emphasize that after asking God for strength, we'd better put it to use.

As we travel our own paths, we join with the author of Hebrews in affirming, "Jesus Christ is the same yesterday, today, and forever. . . . [Our] strength comes from God's grace."

Lord Jesus, I bring all my doubts to you and all the concerns that cause me such distress. Thank you for the assurance that your favor doesn't depend on the depth of my belief. Please comfort me and strengthen me—and help me to act on the strength you provide.

IGNORANCE AND LITTLE-FAITH

An energetic young man named Ignorance came into the path by a little crooked lane from the country of Conceit. He told Christian and Hopeful he was going to the Celestial City, and would gain admittance at the gate "as other good people do." He saw no need for repentance or reconciliation with God, although the pilgrims tried to help him understand his true condition. He would later fail to enter the Celestial City.

As the pilgrims continued their journey, Christian told Hopeful about Little-faith, a good man who lived in the town of Sincere. One day, three rogues named Faint-heart, Mistrust, and Guilt spied him, rushed up, and demanded his money.

Little-faith turned white and had no strength to fight or flee. "Thieves! Thieves!" he cried.

With that, Guilt clubbed him on the head, knocking him flat on the ground. As he lay there bleeding, the bandits heard someone coming. Fearing it was Great-grace from the city of Good-confidence, they fled.

Christian explained that although Little-faith's mind was set on things divine, his faith was small. Hopeful asked why he wasn't braver when the rogues attacked.

"As for a great heart," Christian replied, "Little-faith had none."

He went on to say some pilgrims have great faith and some little. "Even such champions of the faith as David and Hezekiah were forced to fight these same fellows and were beaten up by them. At one point Peter went up against them, but . . . they handled him so skillfully that at last they made him afraid of a weak girl."

"Let us never . . . brag as if we could do better," Christian said. "I have been in the battle before; and . . . I cannot boast of my own bravery."

When we hear of someone's weakness or cowardice in battles of adversity, it's easy to imagine how we would be stronger and braver in similar circumstances. When we read of the snake in the garden lying to Adam and Eve, it's easy to think we would never be so naïve as to eat the forbidden fruit. Yet, as we journey through life, we learn from our own battles how very human and frail we really are. As pilgrims, we are dependent on God's gifts of courage and discernment to win our battles.

We are called to humility.

In his epistle, James quotes the scripture, "God opposes the proud but gives grace to the humble," and then adds, "so humble yourselves before God." The apostle Peter quotes the same scripture when he writes, "Dress yourselves in humility as you relate to one another, for 'God opposes the proud but gives grace to the humble.'" God's favoring the humble is why we should serve each other.

When our circumstances are easier, or when we have not fallen as some have, or when we see others who can't seem to climb out of a hopeless situation, it's well to remember, "There, but for the grace of God, go I."

Throughout the Bible, we find that God favors the humble. "You rescue the humble," writes the psalmist, "but you humiliate the proud." In Psalm 51 we read, "The sacrifice you desire is a broken spirit. You will not reject a broken and repentant heart, O God."

When we read about Christian's foolishness and failures, we may be tempted to think, *I wouldn't make those same mistakes. What a slow learner.* And in some ways, he was. Yet, we would be wise to consider, *What is it I am learning only too slowly?*

Jesus taught that "those who exalt themselves will be humbled, and those who humble themselves will be exalted."

Father and Creator, thank you for all the magnificence of your creation—including the insights and abilities you've given me. Help me, I pray, to use them wisely, in humility, with a spirit of responsibility and thanksgiving.

THE FALSE ANGEL OF LIGHT

At an intersection of two pathways, Christian and Hopeful encountered a man in a very light robe who asked why they were standing there. They told him they were going to the Celestial City, but weren't sure which of the two paths to take.

"Follow me," said the man, "for that is where I am going."

They followed him down the path that had just intersected with the road, which gradually turned. Still, they kept on following him. But before they realized what had happened, he led them into a net and they became entangled.

The white robe fell off the man's back, and Christian suddenly understood who he was.

"I see what I did wrong," Christian lamented. "Didn't the Shepherds tell us to beware of flatterers?"

"They gave us a map," Hopeful said, "but we forgot to read it."

In their distress, a Shining One appeared. He told them the man who led them into the net was Flatterer, "a false apostle, who has transformed himself into an angel of light."

The Shining One cut the men free. Then he chastised them for not looking at the map and for ignoring the Shepherds' warnings. They went on their way, chastened and wary.

Soon, they met up with Atheist. He laughed at them when they said they were going to Mount Zion. "The place you dream about does not exist anywhere in the world!" he said. "I heard about this place, and . . . I have been seeking this city for twenty years and I know no more about it than I did the first day I set out. . . . But finding nothing . . . I am going back again."

"Is what this man says true?" Christian asked Hopeful.

"No Mount Zion!?" Hopeful exclaimed. "Why, did we not we see the gate of the city from the Delectable Mountains? And besides, are we not to walk by faith? Let us move on."

And so they did. But when they came to the Enchanted Ground, where the air made them drowsy, it was Hopeful who was tempted to nap.

"Do you not remember that one of the Shepherds told us to beware of the Enchanted Ground?" Christian warned.

"Had I been here alone, I would have risked the danger," Hopeful admitted. "I see that what the wise man said is true, 'Two are better than one.'"

The pilgrims had a wealth of instructions and resources to draw on, and their faith experiences had validated the truth of what they had heard and seen. Yet when they were faced with new challenges, they seemed to forget what was most important.

Decades ago, musician Paul Simon wrote a song titled "Slip Slidin' Away." The lyrics lament that the closer you are to your destination, the more you're slip slidin' away. With brief vignettes, Simon sketches ordinary men and women with fears and regrets, but only God knows what's going on in their lives. The Lord's plan is "unavailable to the mortal man."

Many of us resonate with Simon's song. Why are our lives so complicated and disappointing? Are other paths okay after all? Is what we believe about God and heaven real? Are we all just slip slidin' away?

As we move toward our ultimate destination, we encounter people whose deceptive white robes fall off, and we meet others who mock our faith. It's not hard to become perplexed.

When our feet start to slip slide on the path, we need to do what the pilgrims neglected to do—look at the map. The Scriptures inform, challenge, and renew. And we need to beware of flatterers and seductions of all kinds.

Most of all, we need to call on the Lord in humility.

Whatever our spiritual or intellectual turmoil, God's invitation stands: "Call to me and I will answer you and tell you great and unsearchable things you do not know."

Jesus said, "Come to me, all of you who are weary and carry heavy burdens."

Heavenly Father, sorting through the meaning and significance of all the troubles around me—and throughout the world—is far beyond me. Help me to remember to follow the wisdom and direction of Scripture, your divine map. Let me see every decision I face through your eyes, and let me move at the impulse of your love.

BEULAH LAND

After crossing the Enchanted Ground, the pilgrims entered the country of Beulah, where the air was sweet and pleasant. They found comfort and restoration there. Flowers bloomed, birds sang, and the sun shone, for the land was beyond the Valley of the Shadow of Death and out of the reach of Giant Despair. They were on the borders of heaven and could see the city.

Shining Ones walked by. They could hear voices from the Celestial City.

As they got closer, they had a more perfect view. The city was built of pearls and precious stones, and the streets were paved with gold. The reflection of the sun on the city was so glorious they could not look at it directly.

As they continued toward it, they were met by two men in clothes that shone like gold and whose faces shone like light. "You have only two more difficulties to deal with," they said, "and then you will be in the city."

Between them and the gate was a river, but there was no bridge across it. The river was very deep. At the sight, the pilgrims were stunned.

"You must go through," said the Shining Ones, "or you cannot get to the gate."

The pilgrims then, especially Christian, began to despair. They looked this way and that way, in every direction, but they could find no way to escape the river.

The river. We all must cross it. Each of us lives on heaven's edge, a mere breath away.

Preacher Jonathan Edwards could have been summarizing *The Pilgrim's Progress* when he said, "To go to heaven—fully to enjoy God—is infinitely better than the most pleasant accommodations here."

Yet the river is mysterious. We are given many promises about it, but wonder what will happen when we are in it.

We may recall the words of the old spiritual, "Deep river, my home is over Jordan. Deep river, Lord . . . Oh, don't you want to go to the gospel feast . . . where all is peace?" Yes, we do want to be where all is peace. And we may also sing, "I looked over Jordan and what did I see? . . . A band of angels coming after me . . . Swing low, sweet chariot, coming for to carry me home."

We want a gospel feast and to some day see a sweet chariot with welcoming angels. Yet the river we must cross to get there is deep.

Wolfgang Amadeus Mozart wrote some of the most angelic music created, but he also said this: "I thank my God for graciously granting me the opportunity of learning that death is the key which unlocks the door to our true happiness."

Another genius, Dante Alighieri, said, "Heaven wheels above you, displaying to you her eternal glories, and still your eyes are on the ground."

Eyes on the ground. Eyes on the river. That was Christian's problem.

Dying may be quick, or it may be painfully prolonged. Christian, as we shall see, was horrified by it. Yet, whatever our experience crossing the Jordan, God will not forsake us.

Jesus said, "There is more than enough room in my Father's home. If this were not so, would I have told you that I am going to prepare a place for you?"

Lord Jesus, please wash away all dread I may feel about leaving this life. Grant me glimpses of the joy and glory ahead. Help me to live today with a sense of your majesty, love, and care.

TERROR
IN THE RIVER

When they waded into the water of the river, Christian began to sink. He cried out to Hopeful that the waves were going over his head.

"Have courage, my brother," Hopeful challenged, "for I feel the bottom, and it is solid."

Great darkness and horror fell upon Christian.

"Ah, my friend," he moaned, "the sorrows of death surround me." He couldn't remember or speak of the blessings of his pilgrimage, but was focused on his terrible fears that he would die in the river and never enter the gate. He remembered sins he had committed, and he was troubled by visions of demons and evil spirits.

Hopeful did all he could to keep Christian's head above water. He tried to comfort him, saying, "Brother, I see the gate, and there are men waiting to receive us."

"It's you," Christian said. "It is you they wait for."

"These troubles you are going through in these waters are not a sign that God has forsaken you," Hopeful responded. Then he encouraged Christian, reminding him that Jesus Christ had made him whole.

At that, Christian cried out with a loud voice, "Oh! I see him again, and he tells me, 'When you pass through the waters, I will be with you; and through the rivers, they shall not overflow you.'"

Christian found ground to stand on, and the rest of the river was shallow. Then they crossed over.

We never know just how we'll react when we get right up to the river or feel ourselves sucked into its currents. When we face death, will we be like Christian? Or will we be like Hopeful, who kept his mind set on God's promises?

Christian was full of terrible fears about his failures and sins. Had he concentrated instead on the celebration of grace the Word proclaims, his fears may have been allayed. He might have taken courage from the words of the apostle Paul, who contrasts sin with "God's wonderful grace and gift of forgiveness." Everyone who receives his grace "will live in triumph over sin and death."

Several of Paul's epistles begin with this greeting, "May God the Father and our Lord Jesus Christ give you grace and peace." That's the Good News, the "generous grace" of God. Jesus spoke of this great gift when he said, "For it is my Father's will that all who see his Son and believe in him should have eternal life."

As the river's waves came over Christian, he was plagued by his wretchedness. He might instead have called upon the hope of John Newton's beloved lyrics, "Amazing grace! How sweet the sound that saved a wretch like me! . . . 'Twas grace that taught my heart to fear, and grace my fears relieved."

Christian momentarily lost sight of God's sweet grace.

At Jordan's edge, or floundering in its fearsome currents, we have this encouragement from the apostle Paul: "Now may our Lord Jesus Christ himself and God our Father, who loved us and by his grace gave us eternal comfort and a wonderful hope, comfort you and strengthen you." It truly is grace that has brought us safe this far, and grace that will lead us home.

Just months before his own death, C. S. Lewis wrote this to a friend with a terminal illness: "Can you not see death as the friend and deliverer? . . . What is there to be afraid of? . . . Your sins are confessed. . . . There are better things ahead than any we leave behind. . . . Don't you think Our Lord says to you, 'Peace, child, peace. Relax. Let go. Underneath are the everlasting arms. Let go, I will catch you.'"

Father in heaven, I never want to lose sight of your sweet grace. Thank you for your eternal comfort and wonderful hope. I praise you and thank you for your gift of salvation and for your promise of a warm welcome beyond the river.

THE GLORIOUS WELCOME

Two Shining Men were waiting for Christian and Hopeful. Their mortal garments were left behind in the river, and they climbed up with agility and speed. They talked happily as they went. Clouds were their chariots and angels their guides.

"You are going now to the paradise of God," the Shining Ones said, "where you will see the tree of life and eat of its never-fading fruits; and there you will have white robes given you, and you will walk and talk every day with the King. . . . You will never again see such things as sorrow, sickness, affliction, and death."

"What shall we do in the holy place?" the pilgrims asked.

"You shall serve continually, with praise, shouting, and thanksgiving. . . . There your eyes shall be delighted with seeing, and your ears with hearing the pleasant voice of the Mighty One. There you shall enjoy your friends again who have gone before you. . . . There you shall be clothed with glory and majesty, and shall ride out with the King of Glory."

As they neared the gate, a company of the heavenly host came out to meet them and gave a great shout: "Blessed are they which are called into the marriage supper of the Lamb."

The King's trumpeters, clothed in white and shining clothes, made the heavens echo with melodious sounds. Bells rang to welcome them.

As Christian and Hopeful went through the gate, they were transfigured and clothed in garments that shone like gold.

The bells rang again, and they were told, "Enter ye into the joy of your Lord."

Biblical visions of heaven inspire us with celebrations and the ultimate joy of coming "home at last." We will be with Jesus, who prayed, "Father, I want these whom you have given me to be with me where I am. Then they can see all the glory you gave me because you loved me even before the world began!"

In heaven, we will be filled with the Holy Spirit. We will be praising God.

What else will we be doing? We might envision that God's creative wonders will be multiplied. If we found earth chock-full of stunning marvels, why wouldn't we be in for even greater adventures of discovery in the next life—adventures literally unimaginable? After all, "when we've been there 10,000 years," we'll have only just begun!

And we will have new bodies in which to do wonderful things. Joni Eareckson Tada, who lost the use of her limbs in a diving accident, will finally be dancing. Helen Keller, left blind and deaf by childhood illness, will see and hear again. She wrote, "For three things I thank God every day of my life: thanks that he has vouchsafed me knowledge of his works; deep thanks that he has set in my darkness the lamp of faith; deep, deepest thanks that I have another life to look forward to—a life joyous with light and flowers and heavenly song."

In many ways, we're all in the dark like Helen Keller, needing the lamp of faith and the promise of heaven. But for many, academia and the media have largely smothered that lamp. Scholar Jeffrey Burton Russell, a self-described "lapsed atheist," writes in his *Paradise Mislaid*, "Heaven has gradually been shut away in a closet by the dominant intellectual trends." He goes on to chronicle "how we lost heaven" and what we must do to regain it.

Heaven is not a fantasy. We need it as a ship in a storm needs the light of a lighthouse. And in 1 Corinthians 2 we have this description of the unimaginable that awaits us:

> *"No eye has seen, no ear has heard,*
>   *and no mind has imagined*
> *what God has prepared*
>   *for those who love him."*

Father in heaven, you know it's hard for me at times to be hopeful and confident of your welcome in the next life. I realize I can't create my own hope! I can't create my own confidence in your promises. Help me to get my eyes off my troubles and doubts. Fill me with hope and joy as I anticipate the promise of coming home to you and participating in your unimaginable adventures there.

PART 2

The
PILGRIM'S
PROGRESS

BY
JOHN BUNYAN

CONTENTS

As I walked through the wilderness of this world, I came upon a certain place where there was a den, and I laid down in that place to sleep: and as I slept I dreamed a dream. In my dream I saw a man dressed in rags standing with his face turned away from his own house; he held a book in his hand and carried a great burden upon his back. I saw the man open the book and read; and as he read, he wept and trembled and cried out mournfully, "What shall I do?"

In this distraught condition the man went home, determined not to say anything to his family, for he did not want them to see his distress; but he could not be silent long because he was so greatly troubled. Finally he told his wife and children what was on his mind: "O my dear wife and children," he said, "I am greatly troubled by a burden that lies heavy upon me. Moreover, I have been informed that our city will be burned with fire from heaven; and in this fearful destruction both myself and you, my wife and my sweet children, shall perish, unless we can find some way of escape or deliverance, which presently I cannot see."

His family was amazed at his words. Not because they believed what he said, but because they thought he was mentally deranged. Since it was almost night, and they hoped that sleep might settle his mind, they got him to bed as quickly as they could. But the night was as troublesome to him as the day; instead of sleeping, he lay awake sighing and crying, so that when morning came and they asked him how he felt, he told them, "Worse and worse." He began talking to them in the same vein again. Thinking they could drive away his madness with harsh behavior, they began to make fun of him, to scold him, and sometimes even to ignore him. Because of this, he began to retire to his room to pray for and pity them, as well as grieve over his own misery; he would also walk alone in the fields, sometimes reading and sometimes praying. For several days he spent his time this way.

Now in my dream I saw that one day when he was walking in the fields, he was reading his book and was greatly distressed; and as he read, he cried out, as he had done before, "What shall I do to be saved?"

> *Christian no sooner leaves the world but meets*
> *Evangelist, who lovingly him greets*
> *With tidings of another; and doth show*
> *Him how to mount to that from this below.*

He looked this way and that, as if he wanted to run but did not know which way to go. Then I saw a man named Evangelist coming toward him. "Why are you crying?" Evangelist asked.

The man answered, "Sir, this book tells me I am condemned to die, and after that to come to judgment, and I find that I am not willing to do the first, nor able to do the second."

Then said Evangelist, "Why are you not willing to die, since this life is filled with so many evils?" The man answered, "Because I fear that this burden that is upon my back will sink me lower than the grave, and I shall fall into hell. And, sir, I am not fit to go to judgment, and from there to execution; and the thought of these things makes me cry."

Then said Evangelist, "If this is your condition, why are you standing here?" The man answered, "Because I don't know where to go." Then Evangelist gave him a parchment roll, upon which was written, "Flee from the wrath to come."

The man read it and, looking at Evangelist very carefully, said, "Where shall I go?" Evangelist pointed across a very wide field, "Do you see that wicket-gate over there?" The man said, "No." Then said Evangelist, "Do you see that shining light over there?" The man said, "I think I do." Then said Evangelist, "Keep your eyes on that light and go directly to it; then you will see the gate. Knock on it, and you will be told what you should do."

So I saw in my dream that the man began to run. Now, he had not run far from his own door when his wife and children saw him and began to cry for him to return; but the man put his fingers in his ears and ran on, crying, "Life! Life! Eternal life!" So he did not look behind him, but fled toward the middle of the plain.

The neighbors also came out to watch him run; some mocked him, others threatened, and some called for him to return. Among those who called to him were two men who resolved to fetch him back by force. The name of the one was Obstinate, and the name of the other was Pliable.

Now by this time the man had gotten a good distance from them; but they were resolved to pursue him, which they did, and in a little while they overtook him. Then said the man, "Neighbors, why have you come?" They said, "To persuade you to go back with us." But he said, "You cannot do that. You dwell in the City of Destruction, the place where I was born; and if you die there, sooner or later, you will sink lower than the grave into a place that burns with fire and brimstone. Be content, good neighbors, and go along with me."

OBSTINATE: What! And leave our friends and our comforts behind us?

"Yes," said Christian (for that was the man's name), "because ALL that you shall forsake is not worthy to be compared with a little of that which I am seeking; and if you will go with me, you shall fare as I do, for where I go there is enough and more to spare. Come with me and see that I speak the truth."

OBSTINATE: What are you seeking, since you leave all the world to find it?

CHRISTIAN: I seek an inheritance that can never perish, spoil, or fade, and it is kept in heaven, to be bestowed, at the time appointed, on those who diligently seek it. Read about it in my book.

OBSTINATE: Nonsense! I don't care about your book. Will you go back with us or not?

CHRISTIAN: No, I will not, because I have put my hand to the plow.

OBSTINATE: Come then, neighbor Pliable, let us turn back and go home without him. Crazy fools like this are so conceited that they think they are wiser than seven men who can give good reasons why they are wrong.

PLIABLE: Don't be unkind. If what the good Christian says about the things he seeks is true, I am inclined to go with him.

OBSTINATE: What! Another fool! Take my advice and go back. Who knows where such a mad fellow will lead you? Be wise and go back home.

CHRISTIAN: No, come with me, Pliable. The things I have told you about are waiting, as well as many more wonderful things. If you don't believe me, read here in this book; and the truth of what is said here is confirmed by the blood of Him who wrote it.

PLIABLE: Well, neighbor Obstinate, I believe I will go along with this good man and cast in my lot with him; but, my good companion, do you know the way to this desired place?

CHRISTIAN: I have been told by a man whose name is Evangelist to go to a little gate that is before us, where we shall receive instructions about the way.

PLIABLE: Come then, good neighbor, let us be going.

Then the two went on together.

OBSTINATE: And I will go back home. I will not be a companion to such misled, foolish fellows.

Now I saw in my dream that when Obstinate had left, Christian and Pliable went across the plain together talking.

CHRISTIAN: Neighbor Pliable, I am glad you have decided to go along with me. Had Obstinate felt what I have felt of the powers and terrors of what is yet unseen, he would not have turned his back on us so lightly.

PLIABLE: Come, neighbor Christian, since there are only the two of us here now, tell me now about where we are going and the things we will enjoy there.

CHRISTIAN: I can better imagine them with my mind than speak of them with my tongue; but since you want to know, I will read to you from my book.

PLIABLE: And do you think that the words of your book are really true?

CHRISTIAN: Yes, certainly; for it was written by him who cannot lie.

PLIABLE: Well said. So tell me more about this place.

CHRISTIAN: There is an endless kingdom to be inhabited, and we will be given everlasting life so we may inhabit that kingdom forever.

PLIABLE: Well said. And what else?

CHRISTIAN: We will be given crowns of glory and garments that will make us shine like the sun.

PLIABLE: This sounds very pleasant. And what else?

CHRISTIAN: There shall be no more crying nor sorrow in that place where we are going; for he who is owner of the place will wipe all tears from our eyes.

PLIABLE: And who else will be there?

CHRISTIAN: There we shall be with seraphim and cherubim, creatures that will dazzle your eyes. There also you shall meet with thousands and ten thousands who have gone before us to that place. None of them are unkind, but are loving and holy; every one walks in the sight of God and stands in his presence with acceptance forever. There we shall see the elders with their golden crowns; the holy virgins with their golden harps; and the men and women who by the world were cut in pieces, burnt in flames, eaten by beasts, drowned in the seas, because of the love that they have for the Lord of that place. All of them will be well and clothed with immortality.

PLIABLE: Just hearing about this is enough to delight one's heart. But how shall we get to share in these things and enjoy them?

CHRISTIAN: The Lord, the Governor of the country to which we are going, has recorded that in this book. The substance of it is that if we are truly willing to have all this, he will bestow it upon us freely.

PLIABLE: I am glad to hear these things. Let us hurry.

CHRISTIAN: I cannot go as fast as I would like because of this burden on my back.

Now I saw in my dream, that just as they had finished this conversation, they came to a very miry swamp that was in the middle of the plain; and because they were not paying attention to where they were walking, they both fell into a bog called the Swamp of Despond. Here they floundered for a time, covered with mud; and Christian, because of the burden on his back, began to sink in the mire.

PLIABLE: Ah! neighbor Christian, where are you now?

CHRISTIAN: Truly, I do not know.

At that Pliable began to be displeased and angrily said to Christian, "Is this the happiness you've been telling me about all this time? If we're having this much trouble at the start, what can we expect between here and our journey's end? If I get out of this place alive, you can go on without me." And with that Pliable gave a desperate struggle or two and got himself out of the mire on the side of the swamp that was nearest to his own house, and Christian saw him no more.

Now Christian was left to flounder in the Swamp of Despond alone. But still he managed to make it to that side of the swamp that was farthest from his own house and next to the wicket-gate, although he could not get out because of the burden upon his back.

Then I saw in my dream that a man, whose name was Help, came to him and asked him, "What are you doing there?"

CHRISTIAN: Sir, I was told to go this way by a man called Evangelist, who directed me also to yonder gate, that I might escape the wrath to come; and as I was going toward it, I fell in here.

HELP: But why did you not look for the steps?

CHRISTIAN: I was so afraid that I wasn't paying attention and I fell in.

Then said Help, "Give me your hand." So Christian gave him his hand, and Help drew him out and set him upon firm ground and told him to go on his way.

hen I stepped to Help, who had pulled Christian out, and said, "Sir, since this is the way from the City of Destruction to yonder gate, why is it that this piece of ground is not repaired so that poor travelers might go this way with more security?"

And Help said to me, "This miry swamp cannot be repaired. It is where the scum and filth of the conviction of sin collects, and therefore it is called the Swamp of Despond; for as the sinner becomes aware of his lost condition, many fears and doubts and discouraging apprehensions arise in his soul; and all of them together settle in the depths of this place. And this is the reason for the bad condition of this ground.

"It is not the desire of the King that this place should remain in such a state. For over sixteen hundred years his laborers have, at the direction of his Majesty's surveyors, been working on this patch of ground. Yes, and to my knowledge," said Help, "at least twenty thousand cartloads—yes, millions of wholesome instructions—have been swallowed up here. They that are knowledgeable say they are the best materials to make good ground of the place. But it is still the Swamp of Despond, and will be when they have done what they can.

"True, at the direction of the Lawgiver, certain good and substantial steps have been placed through the very midst of this swamp. But during the times when this place spews out its filth, these steps can hardly be seen; or if they are, men become confused and overstep them and become mired down, even though the steps are there. But once they get to the gate, the ground is good."

Now I saw in my dream that by this time Pliable had returned to his home, where his neighbors came to visit him; and some of them called him a wise man for coming back, and some called him a fool for hazarding himself with Christian. Others mocked him for his cowardliness, saying, "Surely, since you began the venture, you should not have turned back because of a few difficulties. I would not have done so." So Pliable sat cringing among them. But eventually, when he gained more confidence, they all changed their tune and began to deride poor Christian behind his back. And thus we leave Pliable.

Now as Christian was walking by himself, he spied someone afar off coming across the field toward him, and before long their paths crossed. This gentleman's name was Mr. Worldly Wiseman, and he lived in the town of Carnal Policy, a large town located near where Christian had come from.

Thus, this man knew about Christian, for there had been much talk about his setting forth from the City of Destruction, not only in that place where he had lived, but in nearby towns. Master Worldly Wiseman, therefore, having some ideas about him after observing his difficult path and his sighs and groans, began to converse with him.

WORLDLY WISEMAN: Hello, my good man, where are you going in this burdened manner?

CHRISTIAN: A burdened manner indeed, and as great as any poor creature ever had! And since you ask me where I'm going, I tell you, sir, I am going to yonder wicket-gate; for there, so I have been told, I shall be able to get rid of my heavy burden.

WORLDLY WISEMAN: Have you a wife and children?

CHRISTIAN: Yes, but this burden loads me down so that I cannot enjoy them as I once did; it is as if I had none.

WORLDLY WISEMAN: Will you listen to me if I give you some advice?

CHRISTIAN: If it is good, I will, for I stand in need of good counsel.

WORLDLY WISEMAN: I would advise you, then, to get rid of your burden quickly, for until you do, you will never be settled in your mind, nor will you be able to enjoy the benefits of the blessing which God has bestowed upon you.

CHRISTIAN: That is what I am seeking: to get rid of this heavy burden. But I cannot get it off myself, nor is there any man in our country who can take it off my shoulders. Therefore I am going this way, as I told you, to get rid of my burden.

WORLDLY WISEMAN: Who told you to go this way to get rid of your burden?

CHRISTIAN: A man who appeared to me to be a very great and honorable person. His name was Evangelist.

WORLDLY WISEMAN: I condemn him for his advice, for there is no more dangerous and troublesome way in the world than that to which he has directed you, and that you will find if you heed his counsel. You have met with something already, I perceive, for I see the dirt of the Swamp of Despond upon you. But that swamp is just the beginning of the trouble that awaits those who go that way. Hear me! I am older than you. If you continue on, you are likely to meet with weariness, pain, hunger, perils, nakedness, sword, lions, dragons, darkness, and, in a word, death! These things have been confirmed by many testimonies. So why should you carelessly throw your life away on the word of a stranger?

CHRISTIAN: Why, sir, this burden upon my back is more terrible to me than all those things you have mentioned. No, I don't care what I encounter on the way if I can be delivered from my burden.

WORLDLY WISEMAN: How did you get this burden in the first place?

CHRISTIAN: By reading this book in my hand.

WORLDLY WISEMAN: I thought so! It has happened to you as it has to other weak men, who, meddling with things too high for them, do suddenly fall into confusion as you have. Such confusion not only unnerves men, as it has done with you, but sends them on desperate paths seeking they know not what.

CHRISTIAN: I know what I seek: it is ease for my heavy burden.

WORLDLY WISEMAN: But why do you search for ease along this dangerous path? Especially since, if you have patience to hear me out, I can direct you to what you desire without the dangers that you will run into in this way. Yes, the solution is at hand, and it does not involve those dangers. Instead, you will meet with much safety, friendship, and content.

CHRISTIAN: Pray, sir, tell me this secret.

WORLDLY WISEMAN: All right. In that village over there called Morality lives a gentleman named Legality, a very judicious and honorable man who has the skill to help men rid themselves of such burdens as yours. To my knowledge he has done a great deal of good in this way and has the skill to cure those who are somewhat crazed with their burdens. You can go to him for help. His house is not quite a mile from this place, and if he should not be at home himself, his handsome young son, Civility, can help you as well as the old gentleman himself.

There you can be eased of your burden. And if you do not want to go back to your former habitation, as indeed I would not wish you to, you may send for your wife and children to join you in this village, where there are houses available at reasonable rates. Everything you need for a happy life will be provided there, and you will live among honest neighbors.

Now Christian was somewhat at a standstill; but soon he concluded that if what this gentleman said was true, then the wisest course was to take his advice.

CHRISTIAN: Sir, which way do I take to this honest man's house?

WORLDLY WISEMAN: Do you see that high hill over there?

CHRISTIAN: Yes, I see it clearly.

WORLDLY WISEMAN: Go past that hill, and the first house you come to is his.

So Christian turned aside to go to Mr. Legality's house for help. But when he was close to the hill, it seemed so high and hung so far over the path that he was afraid to venture further, lest the hill should fall on his head. Therefore he stood still, not knowing what to do. Also his burden now seemed heavier to him than it had before, and there were flashes of fire coming out of the hill that made Christian afraid he should be burned. He began sweating and quaking with fear.

> *When Christians unto carnal men give ear*
> *Out of their way they go, and pay for it dear;*
> *For Master Worldly Wiseman can but show*
> *A saint the way to bondage and to woe.*

Now Christian began to be sorry that he had taken Mr. Worldly Wiseman's counsel. And with that he saw Evangelist coming to meet him and began to blush with shame. Evangelist drew nearer and nearer; and when he came up to Christian, he looked at him with a severe and fearsome expression. Then he began to reason with Christian.

EVANGELIST: What are you doing here, Christian?

Christian didn't know what to say, so he stood speechless before him.

EVANGELIST: Aren't you the man I found crying outside the walls of the City of Destruction?

CHRISTIAN: Yes, dear sir, I am the man.

EVANGELIST: Didn't I tell you the way to the little wicket-gate?

CHRISTIAN: Yes, dear sir.

EVANGELIST: How is it, then, that you have so quickly turned aside? For you are now going the wrong way.

CHRISTIAN: As soon as I got out of the Swamp of Despond I met a gentleman who persuaded me that I might find a man who could take off my burden in the village before me.

EVANGELIST: Who was he?

CHRISTIAN: He looked like a gentleman, and talked much to me, and got me at last to yield, so I came here. But when I saw this hill and how it hangs over the path, I suddenly stopped, lest it should fall on my head.

EVANGELIST: What did that gentleman say to you?

CHRISTIAN: Why, he asked me where I was going, and I told him.

EVANGELIST: And what did he say then?

CHRISTIAN: He asked me if I had a family, and I told him I did. But I told him I was so loaded down with the burden on my back that I cannot take pleasure in them as I did formerly.

EVANGELIST: And what did he say then?

CHRISTIAN: He told me to get rid of my burden quickly, and I said I wanted to and was going to yonder gate to receive further direction on how I may get to the place of deliverance. He said that he would show me a better and shorter and less difficult way than that which you told me about, sir. He said he would direct me to a gentleman who has skill to take off these burdens; so I believed him. But when I came to this place and saw things as they are, I stopped because I was afraid it was dangerous. Now I don't know what to do.

Then Evangelist said, "Stand still for a bit so I may show you the words of God."

So Christian stood, trembling.

Then said Evangelist, "See that ye refuse not him that speaketh. For if they escaped not who refused him that spake on earth, much more shall not we escape, if we turn away from him that speaketh from heaven." Moreover, he said, "Now the just shall live by faith: but if any man draw back, my soul shall have no pleasure in him." Then he concluded with this application: "Thou art the man who is running into this misery. You have begun to reject the counsel of the Most High and to draw back from the way of peace, almost to the point of perdition."

Then Christian fell down at Evangelist's feet, crying, "Woe is me, for I am undone!"

At the sight of this, Evangelist caught him by the right hand, saying, "All manner of sin and blasphemies shall be forgiven men. Be not faithless, but believing."

Then Christian recovered somewhat and stood up, trembling as he had before, and Evangelist continued speaking.

EVANGELIST: Heed seriously the things that I shall tell you, for I will now show you who it was that deluded you and who it was to whom he was sending you. The man who met you is one Worldly Wiseman, and he is rightly named; partly because he enjoys only the doctrine of this world, which is why he always goes to the town of Morality to church, and partly because he loves that doctrine best, for it saves him from the cross. And because he is of this carnal nature he seeks to pervert my ways, though they are right. Now there are three things in this man's counsel that you must utterly abhor.

First, he turned you out of the way; second, he tried to make the cross odious to you; and third, he set your feet on a path that leads to death.

First, you must abhor his turning you out of the way—yes, and your own consenting to do so—because to do this is to reject the counsel of God for the counsel of a Worldly Wiseman. The Lord says, "Strive to enter in at the strait gate," the gate to which I sent you, for "strait is the gate that leadeth unto life, and few there be that find it." This wicked man has turned you from your pilgrimage to the little wicket-gate, and in doing so has brought you almost to destruction. Hate, therefore, his turning you out of the way, and abhor yourself for listening to him.

Second, you must abhor his attempts to make the cross repugnant to you, for you are to desire the cross more than "the treasure of Egypt." Besides, the King of Glory has told you that he who "will save his life shall lose it" and he who comes after him "and hates not his father, and mother, and wife, and children, and brethren, and sisters, yea, and his own life also, he cannot be my disciple." Therefore, you must abhor any doctrine that would persuade you that this truth, without which you cannot have eternal life, shall be your death.

Third, you must abhor his getting you to take the path that leads to death. And in this regard you must consider to whom he sent you and how unable that person was to deliver you from your burden.

You were sent to Legality, the son of the bond-woman who now is in bondage with her children. This is a mystery, this Mount Sinai, which you feared would fall on your head. Now if she and her children are themselves in bondage, how can you expect them to free you? Legality, therefore, is not able to set you free from your burden. No man has ever yet been relieved of his burden by Legality, nor ever is likely to be. You cannot be justified by works of the law; for the law cannot release any man from his burden. Therefore, Mr. Worldly Wiseman is an alien, and Mr. Legality is a cheat; and his son Civility is nothing but a hypocrite and cannot help you. Believe me, what you have heard from these stupid men is nothing but a design to deceive you by turning you from the way I had sent you.

After this, Evangelist called aloud to the heavens for confirmation of what he had said, and with that there came words and fire out of the mountain under which poor Christian stood that made his hair stand up: "As many as are of the works of the law are under the curse; for it is written, Cursed is every one that continueth not in all things which are written in the book of the law to do them." Now Christian expected nothing but death and began to cry out mournfully, even cursing the moment he had met up with Mr. Worldly Wiseman and calling himself a thousand fools for listening to his counsel. He also was greatly ashamed to think that this gentleman's arguments, flowing only from the flesh, had prevailed with him, causing him to forsake the right way. This done, he applied himself again to Evangelist's words.

CHRISTIAN: Sir, what do you think? Is there hope? May I now go back and go up to the wicket-gate? I am sorry I have heeded this man's counsel, but may my sin be forgiven?

EVANGELIST: Your sin is very great, for by it you have committed two evils: you have forsaken the way that is good and you have taken forbidden paths. Yet the man at the gate will receive you, for he has goodwill for men.

Then Christian prepared to go back, and Evangelist, after he had kissed him, smiled and wished him a successful journey. So Christian hurried on, speaking to no one on the way. He traveled quickly, like one who knows he is on dangerous ground, until he once again reached the place where he had left to follow Mr. Worldly Wiseman's counsel. Thus, in time, Christian got up to the gate, over which was written, "Knock, and it shall be opened unto you."

> *He that will enter in must first without*
> *Stand knocking at the gate, nor need he doubt*
> *That is a knocker but to enter in,*
> *For God can love him and forgive his sin.*

He knocked, therefore, several times, saying:

May I now enter here? Will he within
Open to sorry me, though I have been
An undeserving rebel? Then shall I
Not fail to sing his lasting praise on high.

At last an authoritative person named Goodwill came to the gate and asked who was there, and where he had come from, and what he wanted.

CHRISTIAN: I am a poor burdened sinner. I come from the City of Destruction, but am going to Mount Zion so I may be delivered from the wrath to come. Since I have been informed that this gate is the way to that place, I want to know if you are willing to let me in.

GOODWILL: I am willing with all my heart. And with that he opened the gate.

As Christian was stepping through the gate, Goodwill gave him a pull. Then Christian said, "Why did you do that?"

"A little distance from this gate," said Goodwill, "there is a strong castle, of which Beelzebub is the captain; he and his cohorts shoot arrows at those who come up to this gate, hoping they may die before they can enter in."

Then said Christian, "I rejoice and tremble." And when he was in, Goodwill asked who had directed him there.

CHRISTIAN: Evangelist told me to come here and knock. He said that you, sir, would tell me what I must do.

GOODWILL: An open door is before you, and no man can shut it.

CHRISTIAN: Now I begin to reap the benefits of my hazards.

GOODWILL: But how is it that you came alone?

CHRISTIAN: Because none of my neighbors saw their danger, as I saw mine.

GOODWILL: Did any of them know you were coming?

CHRISTIAN: Yes. First my wife and children saw me and called after me to return; also some of my neighbors did the same. But I put my fingers in my ears and kept going.

GOODWILL: But did none of them follow you and try to persuade you to go back?

CHRISTIAN: Yes, both Obstinate and Pliable. When they saw that they could not prevail, Obstinate went back, reviling me, but Pliable came with me a little way.

GOODWILL: But why did he not come through the gate?

CHRISTIAN: We traveled together until we fell into the Swamp of Despond. Then my neighbor Pliable became discouraged and would not venture further. Wherefore, getting out again on that side nearest to his own house, he told me I should go without him. So he went his way, and I came mine—he after Obstinate, and I to this gate.

GOODWILL: Alas, poor man, is the celestial glory of such little value to him that he figures it is not worth risking a few difficulties to obtain it?

CHRISTIAN: Indeed. I have told the truth about Pliable, and if I should tell the truth about myself, I am no better than he. For while it is true that he went back to his own house, I also turned aside to go in the way of death, being persuaded to do so by the carnal arguments of one Mr. Worldly Wiseman.

GOODWILL: Oh, did he find you? And he would have had you seek the easy way with Mr. Legality. Both of them are deceitful. But did you take his advice?

CHRISTIAN: Yes, as far as I dared. I went to find Mr. Legality, until I thought the mountain that stands by his house would fall on my head; wherefore, I was forced to stop.

GOODWILL: That mountain has been the death of many and will be the death of many more; 'tis well you escaped being dashed in pieces by it.

CHRISTIAN: Why, truly, I do not know what would have become of me there, had not Evangelist met me again in the midst of my gloomy state of mind. It was God's mercy that he came to me again, for otherwise I would never have gotten here. But now I am here—I who deserve death by that mountain rather than to stand thus talking with my Lord; oh, what grace this is to me, that I am still admitted entrance here!

GOODWILL: We make no objections against any, notwithstanding all that they have done before they came here. They "in no wise are cast out." Therefore, good Christian, come a little way with me, and I will teach you about the way you must go. Look before you! Do you see that narrow way? That is the way you must go. It was formed by the patriarchs, prophets, Christ, and his apostles, and it is as straight as a rule can make it. That is the way you must go.

CHRISTIAN: But are there no turnings or windings by which a stranger may lose his way?

GOODWILL: Yes, there are many ways that border upon this, and they are crooked and wide. But you can always distinguish the right way, for it is always straight and narrow.

Then I saw in my dream that Christian asked him if he could not help him take off the burden that was upon his back; for as yet he had not got rid of it, nor could he by any means get it off without help.

GOODWILL: As to your burden, be content to bear it until you come to the place of deliverance, for there it will fall from your back by itself.

Then Christian began to prepare himself for his journey, and Goodwill told him that when he had traveled some distance from the gate, he would come to the house of the Interpreter, at whose door he should knock and who would show him excellent things. Then Christian said good-bye to his friend, and he bid him Godspeed.

Christian went on till he came to the house of the Interpreter, where he knocked over and over; at last someone came to the door and asked who was there.

CHRISTIAN: Sir, I am a traveler, who was told by an acquaintance of the good owner of this house that it would be to my benefit to call here; I would therefore speak with the master of the house.

So he called for the master of the house, who after a little time came to Christian and asked him what he wanted.

CHRISTIAN: Sir, I am a man who has come from the City of Destruction, and am going to Mount Zion; and I was told by the man that stands at the gate, at the head of this way, that if I called here, you would show me excellent things that would be a help to me in my journey.

INTERPRETER: Come in. I will show you that which will be profitable to you.

So he commanded his man to light the candle and bid Christian follow him. He led him into a private room and bid his man open a door. When he had done so, Christian saw the picture of a very grave person hanging upon the wall. He had eyes lifted up to heaven, the best of books in his hand, the law of truth written upon his lips, and the world behind his back. He stood as if he pleaded with men, and a crown of gold hung over his head.

CHRISTIAN: What does this mean?

INTERPRETER: The man who is pictured there is one of a thousand; he can beget children, travail in birth with children, and nurse them himself when they are born. And you see him with his eyes lifted up to heaven, the best of books in his hand, and the law of truth upon his lips to show you that his work is to know and unfold dark things to sinners; even as you also see him standing as if he pleaded with men; and you see the world cast behind him and a crown over his head to show you that because he despises the things that are present, for the love he has for his Master's service, he is sure to have glory for his reward in the next world.

Now, I have showed you this picture first because this man pictured here is the only man whom the Lord of the place where you are going has authorized to be your guide in all the difficult places you may encounter on the way; wherefore, heed what I have showed you and bear in mind what you have seen, lest on your journey you meet with some who pretend to lead you right, but whose way only leads to death.

Then he took Christian by the hand and led him into a very large parlor that was full of dust because it was never swept. After a little while the Interpreter called for a man to sweep, and when he began to do so, the dust flew about so abundantly that Christian almost choked on it. Then said the Interpreter to a young woman who stood nearby: "Bring water here and sprinkle the room"; and when she had done this, it was pleasantly swept and cleansed.

CHRISTIAN: What does this mean?

INTERPRETER: This parlor is the heart of a man who was never sanctified by the sweet grace of the Gospel; the dust is his original sin and inward corruptions that have defiled the whole man. He that began to sweep at first is the Law; but she that brought water and sprinkled it is the Gospel. Now you saw that as soon as the first began to sweep, the dust flew about the room so that it could not be cleaned, and you were almost choked with it; this is to show you that the Law, instead of cleansing the heart (by its working) from sin, does revive, strengthen, and increase sin in the soul, even as it does discover and forbid it, for the Law does not give power to subdue sin.

Again, you saw the young woman sprinkle the room with water, upon which it was cleansed with pleasure; this is to show you that when the sweet and precious influence of the Gospel comes into the heart, then sin is vanquished and subdued and the soul made clean and consequently fit for the King of Glory to inhabit.

Moreover, I saw in my dream that the Interpreter took Christian by the hand and led him into a little room where sat two little children, each one in his chair. The name of the eldest was Passion, and the name of the other Patience. Passion seemed to be very discontented, but Patience was very quiet. Then Christian asked, "Why is Passion discontented?" The Interpreter answered, "Their Governor would have him wait for his best things until the beginning of next year; but Passion wants them all now. Patience, however, is willing to wait."

Then I saw that one came to Passion and brought him a bag of treasure and poured it down at his feet, which Passion then took up rejoicingly and laughed Patience to scorn. But I watched, and it was not long before he had spent it all lavishly and had nothing left but rags.

CHRISTIAN: Explain this matter to me more fully.

INTERPRETER: These two lads are figures: Passion represents the men of this world, and Patience the men of that which is to come. As you have seen, Passion will have all now, this year—that is to say, in this world; so are the men of this world, who must have all their good things now. They cannot wait until next year, that is, until the next world, for their portion of good. That proverb, "A bird in the hand is worth two in the bush," is of more authority with them than are all the Divine testimonies about the good of the world to come. But as you saw, he quickly wasted all and had nothing left except rags; so will it be with all such men at the end of this world.

CHRISTIAN: Now I see that Patience is the wiser in many ways. First, because he waits for the best things. And second, because he will have the glory when the other has nothing but rags.

INTERPRETER: And you may add another, and that is that the glory of the next world will never wear out, whereas the good things of this world are suddenly gone. Therefore, Passion did not have as much reason to laugh at Patience, because he had his good things first, as Patience will have to laugh at Passion, because he had his best things last; for first must give place to last because last will have his time to come; but last gives place to nothing, for there is not another to succeed. He, therefore, who has his portion first must have a time to spend it; but he that has his portion last must have it lastingly; therefore it is said of Dives, "Thou in thy lifetime receivedst thy good things, and likewise Lazarus evil things: but now he is comforted, and thou art tormented."

CHRISTIAN: Then I perceive that it is not best to covet things that are now, but to wait for things to come.

INTERPRETER: You speak the truth. "For the things that are seen are temporal; but the things that are not seen are eternal." Since things present are such near neighbors to our fleshly appetite, and since things to come are such strangers to our carnal sense, therefore the first of these suddenly fall into amity, and a distance continues between the second.

Then I saw in my dream that the Interpreter took Christian by the hand and led him into a place where there was a fire burning against a wall, and someone standing by it, continually casting water upon it to quench it; yet the fire burned higher and hotter.

CHRISTIAN: What does this mean?

INTERPRETER: This fire is the work of grace in the heart, and he who casts water upon it, trying to extinguish it, is the Devil. But let me show you why the fire continues to burn higher and hotter.

So he took Christian around to the backside of the wall, where he saw a man with a vessel of oil in his hand, which he also continually cast, secretly, into the fire.

CHRISTIAN: What does this mean?

INTERPRETER: This is Christ, who continually, with the oil of his grace, maintains the work already begun in the heart; by the means of which, notwithstanding what the Devil can do, the souls of his people prove gracious still. And you saw the man standing behind the wall to maintain the fire, teaching you that it is hard for the tempted to see how his work of grace is maintained in the soul.

I saw also that the Interpreter again took Christian by the hand and led him into a pleasant place, where there was a stately palace, beautiful to behold, and Christian was delighted at the sight. He saw also, upon the top thereof, certain persons walking, clothed all in gold.

Then Christian said, "May we go in there?"

Then the Interpreter led him up toward the door of the palace. At the door stood a great company of men who desired to go in, but dared not; while at a little distance from the door, at a table, with a book and his pen before him, sat a man taking down the name of any who should enter there. He saw also that in the doorway stood many men in armor to protect it, ready to do what hurt and mischief they could to the men that would enter. Now Christian was amazed.

At last, when every man stayed back for fear of the armed men, Christian saw a strong and determined-looking man come up to the man that sat there to write, saying, "Set down my name, sir." And when he had done this, the man drew his sword and put an helmet upon his head and rushed toward the armed men, who attacked him with deadly force; but the man, not at all discouraged, cut and hacked fiercely. So after he had received and given many wounds to those that attempted to keep him out, he cut his way through them all and pressed forward into the palace, at which there was a pleasant voice heard from those who walked upon the top of the palace, saying:

> *Come in, come in;*
> *Eternal glory thou shalt win.*

So he went in and was clothed with garments like theirs. Then Christian smiled and said, "I think I know the meaning of this. Now, let me go from this place."

"No, stay," said the Interpreter, "till I have showed you a little more, and after that you shall go on your way." So he took him by the hand again and led him into a very dark room, where there sat a man in an iron cage.

Now to look at him, the man seemed very sad; he sat with his eyes looking down to the ground, his hands folded together, and he sighed as if his heart was breaking. Then said Christian, "What does this mean?" At which the Interpreter told him to talk with the man.

Then said Christian to the man, "What are you?" The man answered, "I am what I once was not."

CHRISTIAN: What were you once?

MAN: I once professed to be a Christian, both in my own eyes and also in the eyes of others; I once was, as I thought, set for the Celestial City, and had then even joy at the thoughts that I should get there.

CHRISTIAN: But what are you now?

MAN: I am now a man of despair and am shut up in it, as in this iron cage. I cannot get out. Oh, now I cannot!

CHRISTIAN: But how came you to be in this condition?

MAN: I stopped watching and being sober. I allowed my lusts to control me; I sinned against the light of the Word and the goodness of God; I have grieved the Spirit, and he is gone; I tempted the Devil, and he has come to me; I have provoked God to anger, and he has left me; I have so hardened my heart that I cannot repent.

Then said Christian to the Interpreter, "But is there no hope for this man?" "Ask him," said the Interpreter. "No," said Christian, "pray, sir you ask him."

INTERPRETER: Is there no hope, that you must be kept in the iron cage of despair?

MAN: No, none at all.

INTERPRETER: Why, the Son of the Blessed is full of pity.

MAN: I have crucified him afresh, I have despised his person, I have despised his righteousness, I have counted his blood an unholy thing, I have "done despite to the spirit of grace." Therefore I have shut myself out of all the promises, and there now remains nothing for me but fearful threats of certain judgment and fiery indignation, which shall devour me as an adversary.

INTERPRETER: Why did you bring yourself into this condition?

MAN: For the enjoyment of the lusts, pleasures, and profits of this world. But now every one of those things gnaws me like a burning worm.

INTERPRETER: But can't you repent and turn from these things?

MAN: God has denied me repentance. His Word gives me no encouragement to believe otherwise; yea, he himself has shut me up in this iron cage; nor can all the men in the world let me out. O eternity! eternity! how shall I grapple with the misery that I must meet with in eternity!

INTERPRETER: Remember this man's misery and let it be a warning to you.

CHRISTIAN: Well, this is fearful! God help me to watch and be sober and to pray that I may shun the cause of this man's misery! Sir, is it not time for me to go on my way now?

INTERPRETER: Wait until I show you one more thing, and then you shall go on your way.

So he took Christian by the hand again and led him into a chamber, where there was someone rising out of bed; and as he put on his clothing, he shook and trembled.

Then said Christian, "Why does this man tremble like that?" The Interpreter then asked the man to tell Christian the reason. So he began and said, "This night, as I was asleep, I dreamed, and behold the heavens grew very black and it thundered and lightninged so fearfully that it put me into an agony. So I looked up in my dream and saw the clouds rushing and colliding at an unusual rate, upon which I heard a great sound of a trumpet and saw a man sitting upon a cloud, attended by the thousands of heaven; they were all in flaming fire, and the heavens were in a burning flame. Then I heard a voice saying, 'Arise, ye dead, and come to judgment.' And, with that, the rocks were torn apart, the graves opened, and the dead that were in them came forth. Some of them were very glad and looked upward; and some tried to hide themselves under the mountains. Then I saw the man that sat upon the cloud open the book and order the world to draw near. Yet there was, because of a fierce flame issuing out before him, a proper distance between him and them, like the distance between the judge and the prisoners at the bar. I heard it also proclaimed to them that attended the man who sat on the cloud, 'Gather together the tares, the chaff, and the stubble, and cast them into the burning lake.' And with that the bottomless pit opened, just about where I stood, and out of it came an abundance of smoke and coals of fire, with hideous noises. He also said to the same persons, 'Gather my wheat into the granary.' And with that I saw many caught up and carried away into the clouds, but I was left behind. I tried to hide myself, but I could not, for the man that sat upon the cloud kept his eye upon me; my sins also came into my mind, and my conscience accused me on every side. Upon this, I awoke from my sleep."

CHRISTIAN: But what made you so afraid of this sight?

MAN: Why, I thought that the day of judgment had come and that I was not ready for it; but what frightened me most was that the angels gathered up several and left me behind; also the pit of hell opened up just where I stood. My conscience, too, afflicted me; and I thought the Judge had his eye upon me, looking at me with indignation.

Then said the Interpreter to Christian, "Have you considered all these things?"

CHRISTIAN: Yes, and they give me both hope and fear.

INTERPRETER: Well, keep all these things in mind that they may prod you forward in the way you must go.

Then Christian began to prepare himself for his journey, and the Interpreter said, "May the Comforter always be with you, good Christian, to guide you in the way that leads to the City."

So Christian went on his way, saying:

> *Here I have seen things rare and profitable;*
> *Things pleasant, dreadful, things to make me stable*
> *In what I have begun to take in hand;*
> *Then let me think on them, and understand*
> *Wherefore they showed me were, and let me be*
> *Thankful, O good Interpreter, to thee.*

Now I saw in my dream that the highway up which Christian was to travel was fenced on either side with a wall, and that wall was called Salvation. Up this way, therefore, did Christian run, but not without great difficulty because of the load on his back.

He ran until he came to a hill, and upon that hill stood a cross, and at the bottom was a sepulcher. So I saw in my dream that just as Christian came up to the cross, his burden was loosened from his shoulders and fell from his back and began to tumble, and continued to do so until it came to the mouth of the sepulcher, where it fell in, and I saw it no more.

Then Christian was glad and lighthearted and said with a merry heart, "He has given me rest through his sorrow, and life through his death." He stood still a while to look and wonder, for it surprised him that the sight of the cross should thus ease him of his burden. He looked and looked, until the tears streamed down his cheeks.

And as he stood looking and weeping, three Shining Ones came to him and said, "Peace to you." And the first said to him, "Your sins are forgiven"; the second stripped him of his rags and clothed him with a clean garment; and the third placed a mark on his forehead and gave him a roll with a seal upon it, which he told him to look at as he ran, and hand it in at the Celestial Gate. Then they went their way.

> *Who's this? the Pilgrim. How! 'tis very true,*
> *Old things are passed away, all's become new.*
> *Strange! he's another man, upon my word,*
> *They be fine feathers that make a fine bird.*

Then Christian jumped for joy three times and went on, singing:

> *Thus far did I come laden with my sin;*
> *Nor could aught ease the grief that I was in*
> *Till I came hither: What a place is this!*
> *Must here be the beginning of my bliss?*
> *Must here the burden fall from off my back?*
> *Must here the strings that bound it to me crack?*
> *Blest cross! blest sepulcher! blest rather be*
> *The Man that there was put to shame for me!*

I saw then in my dream that Christian went on joyfully until he came to a low-lying place, where he saw, a little out of the way, three men fast asleep with chains upon their feet. The name of the one was Simple, the second Sloth, and the third Presumption.

Christian went to see if perhaps he might wake them, and cried, "You are like those who sleep on top of a mast, for the Dead Sea is under you—a gulf that has no bottom. Awake, therefore, and come away; and if you are willing, I will help you take off your shackles." He also told them, "If he that goes about like 'a roaring lion' comes by, certainly you will become prey for him." With that they looked at him and began to reply in this manner.

Simple said, "I see no danger"; Sloth said, "Let me sleep a little more"; and Presumption said, "I can make it myself without any help from you!" And so they lay down to sleep again, and Christian went on his way. Yet he was troubled to think that men in such danger should think so little of his kindness in freely offering to help them, both by awakening them, counseling them, and offering to help them remove their chains. And as he was troubled about that, he spied two men come tumbling over the wall on the left side of the narrow way; and they hurried to catch up to him. The name of the one was Formalist, and the name of the other Hypocrisy. So, as I said, they drew up to him, and he entered into conversation with them.

CHRISTIAN: Gentlemen, where do you come from and where are you going?

FORMALIST AND HYPOCRISY: We were born in the land of Vain-glory and are going to Mount Zion for the purpose of doing a praiseworthy thing.

CHRISTIAN: Why didn't you enter at the gate which stands at the beginning of the way? Don't you know that it is written that he who does not come in by the door "but climbs up some other way is a thief and a robber"?

FORMALIST AND HYPOCRISY: To go to the gate for entrance is considered too far by all our countrymen. Therefore, the usual way is to take a shortcut and climb over the wall, as we have done.

CHRISTIAN: But won't it be considered a trespass against the Lord of the city where we are going, to thus violate his revealed will?

FORMALIST AND HYPOCRISY: As for that, don't trouble yourself about it; for what we did is according to custom, and we can produce, if need be, testimony that would attest that it has been so for more than a thousand years.

CHRISTIAN: But will your practice hold up in a court of law?

FORMALIST AND HYPOCRISY: That custom, being of so long a standing over a thousand years, would doubtless now be admitted as legal by an impartial judge; and besides, if we get into the way, why does it matter which way we get in? If we are in, we are in. You came in at the gate, and we came tumbling over the wall. In what way is your condition better than ours?

CHRISTIAN: I walk by the rule of my Master; you walk by the ignorant working of your own imagination. You are considered thieves already by the Lord of the way; therefore I doubt that you will be found true men at the end of the way. You come in by yourselves without his direction, and shall go out by yourselves without his mercy.

To this they had little to say, only to tell him to mind his own business. Then I saw that they went on, each in his own way, without much conversation between them, except that these two men told Christian that as far as laws and ordinances were concerned, they thought they should abide by them as conscientiously as he; therefore, they didn't see how he was any different from them except for the coat on his back, which was, they thought, given to him by some of his neighbors to hide the shame of his nakedness.

CHRISTIAN: You will not be saved by laws and ordinances, since you did not come in by the door. And as for this coat on my back, it was given me by the Lord of the place where I am going; and that, as you say, to cover my nakedness with. And I take it as a token of his kindness to me; for I had nothing but rags before. And besides, I comfort myself with this thought as I travel: Surely, I think, when I come to the gate of the city, the Lord will know me since I have his coat on my back—a coat he gave me freely in the day that he stripped me of my rags. I have, moreover, a mark on my forehead, which perhaps you have not noticed, which one of my Lord's most intimate associates placed there on the day that my burden fell off my shoulders. Moreover, at that time I was also given a scroll, sealed, which I can comfort myself by reading as I go on the way; I was also told to turn it in at the Celestial Gate, to assure my admittance. But, I suppose, it is unlikely that you want any of these things because you did not come in at the gate.

They didn't reply to his comments, except to look at each other and laugh. Then I saw that they all went on, but Christian kept in front of them, talking only to himself, sometimes with a sigh and sometimes with assurance; also he often read the scroll that the Shining Ones had given him, and was refreshed by it.

They all went on till they came to the foot of the Hill Difficulty, at the bottom of which was a spring. There were also in the same place two other paths besides that which came straight from the gate; one turned to the left and the other to the right at the bottom of the hill; but the narrow path went right up the hill, and it was called Difficulty. Christian now went to the spring and drank to refresh himself, and then began to go up the hill, saying:

> *The hill, though high, I covet to ascend,*
> *The difficulty will not me offend;*
> *For I perceive the way to life lies here.*
> *Come, pluck up heart, let's neither faint nor fear;*
> *Better, though difficult, the right way to go,*
> *Than wrong, though easy, where the end is woe.*

The other two also came to the foot of the hill; but when they saw that the hill was steep and that there were two other ways to go, and figuring that on the other side of the hill these two paths would meet up with the one Christian had taken, they decided to take those paths. Now the name of one of those ways was Danger, and the name of the other was Destruction. So the one took the way called Danger, which led him into a great wood, and the other took the way to Destruction, which led him into a wide field full of dark mountains, where he stumbled and fell and rose no more.

> *Shall they who wrong begin yet rightly end?*
> *Shall they at all have safety for their friend?*
> *No, no; in headstrong manner they set out,*
> *And headlong will they fall at last, no doubt.*

I then watched Christian go up the hill, where I saw him go from running to walking, and from walking to climbing on his hands and knees, because it was so steep. Now about halfway up the hill was a pleasant shelter covered with trees and vines, provided by the Lord of the hill for the refreshing of weary travelers; and when he got there, Christian sat down to rest. Then he pulled his scroll out and read it for comfort; he also began to think about the coat that was given to him as he stood by the cross. This was all very pleasant, and at last he dozed off, lightly at first and then into a deep sleep, which detained him in that place until it was almost night; and in his sleep his scroll fell out of his hand. Now as he was sleeping, one came to him and woke him, saying, "Go to the ant, thou sluggard; consider her ways, and be wise." And with that Christian suddenly got up and hurried on his way until he came to the top of the hill.

Now when he got up to the top of the hill, two men ran into him at full speed; the name of the one was Timorous and the other Mistrust.

"Sirs, what's the matter?" said Christian. "You are running the wrong way."

"We are going to the City of Zion, and managed to get as far as this difficult place," answered Timorous. "But the further we go, the more danger we meet; so we are turning back."

"Yes," said Mistrust, "for just ahead lie a couple of lions, whether asleep or awake we don't know, but we are certain if we come within their reach they will tear us to pieces."

CHRISTIAN: Your words frighten me, but where can I flee for safety? If I go back to my own country, which faces fire and brimstone, I shall certainly perish there. If I can get to the Celestial City, I am sure to be safe there. I must go forward, facing the risks and dangers. To go back is nothing but death; to go forward is fear of death, and life everlasting beyond it. So I will go forward.

So Mistrust and Timorous ran down the hill, and Christian went on his way. But, thinking again about what he had heard from the men, he reached inside his coat to take out his scroll, that he might read and be comforted; but it was not there. Then Christian was greatly distressed and did not know what to do; for he wanted the scroll that relieved him and that should have been his pass into the Celestial City. Therefore, he became very perplexed about what he should do. At last he remembered that he had slept in the shelter on the side of the hill; and, falling down upon his knees, he asked God's forgiveness for that foolish act, and then he went back to look for his scroll. But all the way back his heart was sorrowful. Sometimes he sighed, sometimes he wept, and often he chided himself for being so foolish as to fall asleep in that place which was erected only for a little refreshment for his weariness. Therefore he went back, carefully looking on both sides all the way, hoping he might find the scroll that had been his comfort so many times on his journey. But when he came within sight of the shelter where he had sat and slept, his sorrow was renewed, for he was reminded again of his wrongdoing. "O wretched man that I am!" he cried. "That I should sleep in the daytime! That I should so indulge the flesh and use that rest to ease my body which the Lord of the hill provided only for the relief of the spirits of pilgrims! How many steps have I taken in vain! (Thus it happened to Israel for their sin; they were sent back again by the way of the Red Sea.) And now I must tread those steps with sorrow which I might have trod with delight, had it not been for this sinful sleep. How far might I have been on my way by this time! Instead, I must tread those steps three times over, instead of only once; yes, now also I will probably be deprived of light, for the day is almost over. Oh, that I had not slept!"

Now by this time he had come to the shelter again, where for a while he sat down and wept; but at last, as God would have it, Christian looked down and saw his scroll underneath a wooden bench, and he quickly picked it up and put it into his coat. But how can words express the joy this man felt when he had gotten his scroll again! For this scroll was his assurance of life and his acceptance at the desired haven. Therefore, he gave thanks to God for directing his eye to the place where it lay, and with joy and tears returned to his journey.

How nimbly he climbed the rest of the hill! Yet before he reached the top, the sun had gone down; and this made him recall the foolishness of his sleeping, and he again became sorrowful. "O thou sinful sleep: because of you, I am deprived of light for my journey! I must walk without the sun; darkness covers the path I must walk; and I must hear the noise of the night creatures because of my sinful sleep." Now he remembered the story that Mistrust and Timorous had told him, how they were frightened by the sight of the lions. Then Christian said to himself, "These beasts range in the night, searching for prey; and if they should meet with me in the dark, how should I escape being torn to pieces?" But while he was bewailing his dangerous situation, he looked up, and behold there was a stately palace before him. The name of it was Beautiful, and it stood right beside the highway.

So I saw in my dream that he hurried forward to see if he might get lodging there. Before he had gone far, he entered a very narrow passage, which was about a furlong from the porter's lodge, and looking very closely at the path ahead, he spied two lions. Now, thought he, I see the dangers that Mistrust and Timorous were driven back by. (The lions were chained, but he did not see the chains.) Then he was afraid, and thought he should go back also, for it seemed nothing but death was before him. But the porter at the lodge, whose name was Watchful, seeing that Christian had stopped as though he might go back, cried out, saying, "Is your strength so small? Do not fear the lions, for they are chained, and are placed there as a trial of faith, and to discover those that have none. Stay in the middle of the path, and no harm shall come to you."

> *Difficulty is behind, fear is before,*
> *Though he's got on the hill, the lions roar;*
> *A Christian man is never long at ease,*
> *When one fright's gone, another doth him seize.*

Then I saw that he went on, trembling for fear of the lions, but heeding carefully the directions of the porter. He heard them roar, but they did him no harm. Then he clapped his hands and went on till he stood before the gate where the porter was. Then said Christian to the porter, "Sir, what house is this? And may I stay here tonight?" The porter answered, "This house was built by the Lord of the hill, and he built it for the relief and security of pilgrims." The porter also asked where he had come from and where he was going.

CHRISTIAN: I come from the City of Destruction and am going to Mount Zion; but because the sun has now set, I would like to stay here tonight if I may.

PORTER: What is your name?

CHRISTIAN: My name is now Christian, but my name used to be Graceless; I came from the race of Japheth, whom God will persuade to dwell in the tents of Shem.

PORTER: But why are you so late? The sun has set.

CHRISTIAN: I would have been here sooner, but "wretched man that I am!" I slept in the shelter on the hillside; even with that, I would have been here much sooner, except that in my sleep I lost my evidence and came without it to the brow of the hill; and then looking for it and not finding it, I was forced to go back to the place where I had slept, where I found it, and now I am here.

PORTER: Well, I will call out one of the virgins, who will, if she likes your words, bring you in to the rest of the family, according to the rules of the house.

So Watchful, the porter, rang a bell, and a grave and beautiful young woman, named Discretion, came out of the house and asked why she had been called.

The porter answered, "This man is journeying from the City of Destruction to Mount Zion, but since he is tired and it is dark, he asked me if he might stay here tonight; so I told him I would call you, who, after speaking with him, would decide, according to the law of the house."

Then she asked him where he was from and where he was going, and he told her. She asked him also how he got into the way; and he told her. Then she asked him what he had seen and met with on the way, and he told her. And last she asked his name, and he said, "It is Christian, and I have an even greater desire to stay here tonight, because, from what I can see, this place was built by the Lord of the hill for the relief and security of pilgrims." She smiled, but there were tears in her eyes; and after a little pause she said, "I will call two or three more of the family." So she ran to the door and called out Prudence, Piety, and Charity, who, after talking with him a little more, had him come in to the family; many of them met him at the threshold of the house and said, "Come in, thou blessed of the Lord; this house was built by the Lord of the hill to entertain pilgrims such as yourself." Then he bowed his head and followed them into the house.

When he had entered and sat down, they gave him something to drink, and they agreed that until supper was ready some of them should have spiritual conversation with Christian, to put their time to the best use; and they appointed Piety and Prudence and Charity to converse with him.

PIETY: Come, good Christian, since we have been kind enough to receive you into our house this night, let us talk with you about all the things that have happened to you in your pilgrimage.

CHRISTIAN: I would be happy to.

PIETY: What caused you to take up the pilgrim's life in the first place?

CHRISTIAN: I was driven out of my native country by something dreadful that I heard; that is, that unavoidable destruction awaited me if I continued to live there.

PIETY: But how did you happen to come out of your country this way?

CHRISTIAN: It was God's doing, for I did not know where to go; but as I was trembling and weeping with fear of destruction, a man named Evangelist happened to come to me, and he directed me to the wicket-gate, which otherwise I should never have found. And thus he set me on the way that has led me directly to this house.

PIETY: But didn't you come past the house of the Interpreter?

CHRISTIAN: Yes, and the memories of the things I saw there will stay with me as long as I live, especially these three things: how Christ, in despite of Satan, maintains his word of grace in the heart; how man's sin is so great that he does not deserve God's mercy; and also the dream of him that dreamed the day of judgment had come.

PIETY: Why, did you hear him tell about his dream?

CHRISTIAN: Yes, and a dreadful one it was. It made my heart ache as he was telling it, and yet I am glad I heard it.

PIETY: Was that all you saw at the house of the Interpreter?

CHRISTIAN: No. He showed me a stately palace, where the people were clad in gold; and while we were there an adventurous man came and cut his way through the armed men who stood in the door to keep him out, and he was told to come in and win eternal glory. I was overcome with joy and delight at the sight of these things and would have stayed at that good man's house a year, except that I knew I had further to go.

PIETY: And what else did you see on the way?

CHRISTIAN: Saw! Why, I had only gone a little further when I saw a man hanging, bleeding, upon a tree, and the very sight of him made my burden fall off my back (for I had been carrying a very heavy burden). I had never seen such a thing before! And while I stood looking up, for then I could not stop looking, three Shining Ones came to me. One of them testified that my sins were forgiven; another stripped me of my rags and gave me this embroidered coat; and the third set the mark that you see on my forehead and gave me this sealed scroll. (And with that he pulled it out of his coat.)

PIETY: But you saw more than this, didn't you?

CHRISTIAN: The things that I have told you were the best; yet there were other things I saw: I saw three men, Simple, Sloth, and Presumption, asleep beside the way, with shackles upon their feet; but do you think I could awake them? I also saw Formality and Hypocrisy come tumbling over the wall, pretending to go to Zion, but they were quickly lost, even as I warned them; but they would not believe. But above all, I found it hard work to get up this hill, and as hard to come past the lions' mouths; and truly if it had not been for the good porter that stands at the gate, I do not know but that I might have turned back after all. But now I thank God I am here, and I thank you for receiving me.

Then Prudence asked him a few questions.

PRUDENCE: Don't you ever think about the country from which you came?

CHRISTIAN: Yes, but with much shame and contempt. If I truly longed for the country I left, I could have returned; but now I desire a better country, that is, a heavenly one.

PRUDENCE: Don't you still bear with you some of the things that concerned you there?

CHRISTIAN: Yes, but greatly against my will, especially inward and carnal thoughts, with which all my countrymen, as well as myself, were delighted. Now all those things are grievous to me, and if I could I would choose never to think of them again; but when I would do that which is best, that which is worst is with me.

PRUDENCE: Don't you find that sometimes those things can be subdued?

CHRISTIAN: Yes, although seldom. But when it happens, it is precious to me.

PRUDENCE: Can you remember by what means you subdue these things that trouble you?

CHRISTIAN: Yes, when I think of what I saw at the cross, that will do it; and when I look upon my embroidered coat, that will do it; and when I look into the scroll that I carry, that will do it; and when I think about where I am going, that will do it.

PRUDENCE: And what is it that makes you so eager to go to Mount Zion?

CHRISTIAN: Why, there I hope to see him alive who was hanging dead on the cross; and there I hope to get rid of all those things that to this day are an annoyance to me; there, they say, there is no death, and there I shall dwell with the kind of companions I like best. For to tell you truth, I love him, because he relieved me of my burden; and I am weary of my inward sickness. I want to be where I shall die no more, and in the company of those who shall continually cry, "Holy, Holy, Holy!" Then Charity said to Christian, "Have you a family? Are you a married man?"

CHRISTIAN: I have a wife and four small children.

CHARITY: Why didn't you bring them along with you?

Then Christian wept and said, "Oh, how willingly I would have done so, but they were all utterly against my going on pilgrimage."

CHARITY: But you should have talked to them and tried to show them the danger of being left behind.

CHRISTIAN: I did. And I told them what God had showed me about the destruction of our city; but I seemed to them "as one that mocked," and they did not believe me.

CHARITY: Did you pray and ask God to bless your advice to them?

CHRISTIAN: Yes, with much love, for you must know that my wife and poor children were very dear to me.

CHARITY: Did you tell them about your own sorrow and fear of destruction?

CHRISTIAN: Yes, over and over and over. They also could see my fears in my expression, in my tears, and in my trembling because of my apprehension about the judgment that hung over our heads; but all that was not sufficient to prevail upon them to come with me.

CHARITY: What did they say for themselves, why they would not come?

CHRISTIAN: Well, my wife was afraid of losing this world, and my children were devoted to the foolish delights of youth; so what with one thing and another, they left me to come this way alone.

CHARITY: Were they perhaps confused because your life did not measure up to your words as you tried to persuade them to come away with you?

CHRISTIAN: Indeed, I cannot commend my life, for I am conscious of my many failings, and I know that a man can damage his witness by bad behavior. Yet this I can say, I was very careful, lest by some unseemly action I would cause them to become averse to going on pilgrimage. In fact, they would tell me I was too precise, and that I denied myself things, for their sakes, in which they saw no evil. No, I think I may say that if they saw anything in me that hindered them, it was my great sensitivity about sinning against God or of doing any wrong to my neighbor.

CHARITY: Indeed Cain hated his brother, "because his own works were evil, and his brother's righteous"; and if your wife and children have been offended by you because of this, they cannot be pleased by goodness, and "thou hast delivered thy soul" from their blood.

Now I saw in my dream that they sat talking together until supper was ready and they sat down to eat. Now the table was set with a feast of rich foods and with good wine, and all their talk at the table was about the Lord of the hill; namely, about what he had done, and why he did what he did, and why he had built that house. And by what they said I perceived that he had been a great warrior and had fought with and slain "him that had the power of death," but not without great danger to himself, which made me love him the more.

For, as they said, and as I believe (said Christian), he did it with the loss of much blood; but that which put the glory of grace into all he did was that he did it out of pure love. And besides, some of the household said they had been with him and spoken with him since he died on the cross; and they attested that they had heard from his own lips that he is such a lover of poor pilgrims that the like is not to be found from the east to the west.

They gave an example of this, and that was that he had stripped himself of his glory so he might do this for the poor; and they had heard him say and affirm that he would not dwell in the mountain of Zion alone. They said, moreover, that he had made princes of many pilgrims who had been born beggars and were by nature destined for the dunghill.

Thus they talked together till late at night; and after they had prayed together for their Lord's protection, they went to bed. They put the pilgrim in a large upper chamber, where the windows opened toward the sunrise. The name of the chamber was Peace, and he slept there till break of day, when he awoke and sang:

> *Where am I now? Is this the love and care*
> *Of Jesus for the men that pilgrims are?*
> *Thus to provide that I should be forgiven!*
> *And dwell already the next door to heaven!*

In the morning they all got up, and after some more conversation, they told Christian that he should not depart till they had shown him the various rooms in the palace. First they took him into the study, where they showed him records of great antiquity; in which, as I remember in my dream, they showed him first the genealogy of the Lord of the hill, that he was the son of the Ancient of Days, and came by that eternal generation. Here also the acts that he had done were more fully recorded, and the names of many hundreds that he had taken into his service; and how he had placed them in habitations that neither time nor death could destroy.

Then they read to him some of the worthy acts that some of his servants had done: how they had "subdued kingdoms, wrought righteousness, obtained promises, stopped the mouths of lions, quenched the violence of fire, escaped the edge of the sword, out of weakness were made strong, waxed valiant in fight, and turned to flight the armies of the aliens."

They then read, in another part of the records of the house, how willing their Lord was to receive anyone into his favor, even those who in the past had defied him. Here Christian also viewed several other histories of famous things, both ancient and modern, together with prophecies and predictions of things to come, both to the dread and amazement of enemies and to the comfort and solace of pilgrims.

The next day they took him into the armory, where they showed him all the equipment their Lord had provided for pilgrims, such as sword, shield, helmet, breastplate, all kinds of prayers, and shoes that would not wear out. And there was enough here to equip as many men for the service of their Lord as there are stars in the heavens.

They also showed him some of the implements with which some of his servants had done wonderful things. They showed him Moses' rod; the hammer and nail with which Jael slew Sisera; the pitchers, trumpets, and lamps with which Gideon put the armies of Midian to flight. Then they showed him the ox's goad with which Shamgar slew six hundred men, the jawbone with which Samson did such mighty feats, the sling and stone with which David slew Goliath, and the sword with which their Lord will kill the Man of Sin. Besides all this, they showed him many excellent things with which Christian was much delighted. This done, they again went to bed.

On the next day he intended to leave, but they wanted him to stay another day. "If the day is clear," they said, "we will show you the Delectable Mountains, which will add to your comfort because they are nearer your destination than this place." So he consented and stayed.

When morning came they took him to the top of the house and told him to look south; so he did, and he saw at a great distance a beautiful mountainous country, with woods, vineyards, fruits and flowers of all sorts, springs and fountains, wonderful to behold. Then he asked the name of the country, and they said, "It is Immanuel's Land, and it belongs to all pilgrims, as does this hill. And when you get there, you will be able to see the gate of the Celestial City."

Now he thought he should leave, and they were willing that he should. "But first," they said, "let us go again into the armory." So they did, and there they equipped him from head to foot in case he should meet with assaults on the way. Being thus clad, he walked out with his friends to the gate, and there he asked the porter if he had seen a pilgrim pass by. The porter answered, "Yes."

CHRISTIAN: Did you know him?

PORTER: He told me his name was Faithful.

CHRISTIAN: Oh, I know him. He comes from the place where I was born and was my neighbor. How far ahead is he?

PORTER: By this time he should be at the foot of the hill.

CHRISTIAN: Well, good Porter, the Lord be with you and bless you greatly for the kindness you have showed to me.

Then he began to go forward, but Discretion, Piety, Charity, and Prudence wanted to accompany him down to the foot of the hill.

So they went on together, discussing their former conversations, till they started down the hill. Then said Christian, "As it was difficult coming up, so, as far as I can see, it is dangerous going down."

"Yes," said Prudence, "so it is, for it is hard for a man to go down into the Valley of Humiliation, as you are now, and not to slip on the way; that is why we came out to accompany you down the hill." So he began to go down, very carefully; yet he did slip a time or two.

Then I saw in my dream that when Christian had gotten to the bottom of the hill, these good companions gave him a loaf of bread, a bottle of wine, and a cluster of raisins. And then he went on his way.

In the Valley of Humiliation poor Christian faced great difficulty, for he had gone only a short distance before he saw a devilish creature named Apollyon coming across the field to meet him. Then Christian began to be afraid and to wonder whether to go back or to stand his ground. But he realized that he had no armor for his back, and should he turn his back he might give the creature a greater advantage, making it easier for the creature to pierce him with his darts. Therefore he resolved to take a chance and stand his ground. "For," he thought, "if I had no more in mind than the saving of my life, it would be the best way to stand."

So he went on, and Apollyon met him. Now the monster was hideous: he was clothed with scales like a fish (and they were his pride); he had wings like a dragon and feet like a bear; out of his belly came fire and smoke; and his mouth was like the mouth of a lion. He looked at Christian with disdain and began to question him.

APOLLYON: Where did you come from and where are you going?

CHRISTIAN: I have come from the City of Destruction, which is the place of all evil, and am going to the City of Zion.

APOLLYON: By this I see that you are one of my subjects, for all that country is mine, and I am the prince and god of it. How is it then that you have run away from your king? If I didn't have hopes that you might serve me further, I would strike you down now with one blow.

CHRISTIAN: Indeed I was born in your dominions, but your service was hard, and your wages such that a man could not live on them, "for the wages of sin is death." Therefore, as I got older I did what other thoughtful persons do: I looked for ways to improve myself.

APOLLYON: No prince takes the loss of his subjects lightly, and I do not want to lose you. But since you have complained about your service and the wages, if you are willing to return, I promise to give you whatever our country can afford.

CHRISTIAN: But I have given myself to another, the King of princes. So how can I with fairness go back with you?

APOLLYON: Like the proverb says, you have "gone from bad to worse." But it is common for those who have professed to be his servants to give him the slip and return again to me. If you do so too, all shall be well.

CHRISTIAN: I have given him my faith and sworn allegiance to him. How can I go back and not be hanged as a traitor?

APOLLYON: You did the same to me, and yet I am willing to overlook it if you will turn now and go back.

CHRISTIAN: What I promised you I did out of youthful innocence and immaturity, and I count on the fact that the Prince under whose banner I stand now is able to absolve me and pardon what I did in compliance to you. And besides, O destroying Apollyon! to tell you the truth, I like his service, his wages, his servants, his government, his company, and his country better than yours. Therefore, stop trying to persuade me further; I am his servant, and I will follow him.

APOLLYON: When you are calmer, consider again what you are likely to encounter along the way you are going. You know, for the most part, his servants come to a bad end because they go against me and my ways. How many of them have been put to shameful deaths! You count his service better than mine, and yet he never came and delivered them from that death. But as for me, how many times, as all the world well knows, have I delivered, either by power or fraud, my faithful servants from him and his, and so I will deliver thee.

CHRISTIAN: At present he purposely does not deliver them in order to prove whether they will be faithful to him to the end; and as for the bad end you say they come to, that is a glorious credit to them. For they do not really expect present deliverance; they wait for the glory they shall have when their Prince comes in his glory with the angels.

APOLLYON: You have already been unfaithful in your service to him. How do you think you will receive wages from him?

CHRISTIAN: Where, O Apollyon, have I been unfaithful to him?

APOLLYON: You lost courage when you first set out and you fell into the Swamp of Despond; then you tried to get rid of your burden in the wrong ways instead of waiting till your Prince had taken it off; you sinfully slept and lost your scroll; you were almost persuaded to go back at the sight of the lions; and when you talk about your journey and what you have heard and seen, inwardly you are seeking your own glory in all that you say and do.

CHRISTIAN: All this is true, and much more that you have left out; but the Prince whom I serve and honor is merciful and ready to forgive. And besides, these failings possessed me in your country, and I have groaned under them, been sorry for them, and have obtained pardon from my Prince.

Then Apollyon broke out into a terrible rage, saying, "I am an enemy of the Prince; I hate him and his laws and his people; I have come out on purpose to oppose you."

CHRISTIAN: Apollyon, beware what you do, for I am on the King's highway, the way of holiness; therefore, take heed.

Then Apollyon straddled the entire path and said, "I have no fear. Prepare to die. For I swear by all my powers that you shall go no further; here will I shed your blood."

And with that he threw a flaming dart at his breast; but Christian had a shield in his hand, with which he caught it and prevented it from striking him.

Then Christian drew back, for he saw it was time to take action; and Apollyon came at him, throwing darts as thick as hail, which, despite all Christian did to avoid them, wounded him in his head, his hand, and his foot. This made Christian fight back. Apollyon therefore continued his attack, and Christian again took courage and resisted as manfully as he could. This combat lasted for over half a day, until Christian was almost exhausted; for Christian's wounds made him grow weaker and weaker.

Then Apollyon, seeing his opportunity, began to close in on Christian, and wrestling with him, gave him a dreadful fall, and Christian's sword flew out of his hand. Then said Apollyon, "I am sure of you now." And with that he had almost pressed him to death, so that Christian began to despair of life. But as God would have it, while Apollyon was preparing to take his last blow, thereby making an end of this good man, Christian nimbly reached out his hand and caught his sword, saying, "Rejoice not against me, O mine enemy; when I fall I shall arise"; and with that gave him a deadly thrust, which made him back away, like someone who had received a mortal wound. When Christian saw this, he went at him again, saying, "Nay, in all these things we are more than conquerors through him that loved us." And with that Apollyon spread his dragon wings and sped away, so that Christian saw him no more for a time.

Unless he had seen it and heard it as I did, no one can imagine this combat: what yelling and hideous roaring Apollyon made during the fight—he sounded like a dragon; and on the other side, what sighs and groans burst from Christian's heart. I never saw him give so much as one pleasant look, till he saw that he had wounded

Apollyon with his two-edged sword; then he did smile and look upward; but it was the most dreadful sight I ever saw.

A more unequal match can hardly be—
Christian must fight an angel; but you see,
The valiant man by handling sword and shield,
Doth make him, though a dragon, quit the field.

So when the battle was over, Christian said, "I will here give thanks to him who has delivered me out of the mouth of the lion, to him who did help me against Apollyon." And so he did, saying:

Great Beelzebub, the captain of this fiend,
Designed my ruin; therefore to this end
He sent him harnessed out: and he with rage
That hellish was, did fiercely me engage.
But blessed Michael helped me, and I
By dint of sword did quickly make him fly.
Therefore to him let me give lasting praise,
And thank and bless his holy name always.

Then there came to him a hand with some of the leaves of the tree of life, which Christian applied to the wounds he had received in the battle and was healed immediately. He also sat down in that place to eat bread and to drink of the bottle that had been given to him earlier. Then being refreshed, he began his journey once more, with his sword drawn; for he said, "Some other enemy may be at hand." But he met with no other attack from Apollyon in this valley.

Now at the end of this valley was another, called the Valley of the Shadow of Death, and Christian had to travel through it because the path to the Celestial City went right through the middle of it. This valley is a very solitary place. Or, as the prophet Jeremiah describes it: "A wilderness, a land of deserts and of pits, a land of drought, and of the shadow of death, a land that no man" (but a Christian) "passed through, and where no man dwelt."

What Christian faced here was worse than his fight with Apollyon, as you shall see.

I saw then in my dream that when Christian got to the borders of the Shadow of Death, he met two men, children of those who brought back an evil report of the Promised Land, and they were hurrying the other way. Christian spoke to them as follows:

CHRISTIAN: Where are you going?

MEN: Back, back! And you should too, if you value either your life or peace.

CHRISTIAN: Why? What's the matter?

MEN: Matter! We were going the same way you are going, and went as far as we dared; and indeed we were almost past the point of no return, for had we gone a little further, we would not be here to bring the news to you.

CHRISTIAN: But what have you met with?

MEN: Why, we were almost in the Valley of the Shadow of Death; but fortunately we happened to look ahead and saw the danger before we came to it.

CHRISTIAN: But what have you seen?

MEN: Seen! Why, the valley itself, which is as dark as pitch; we also saw there the hobgoblins, satyrs, and dragons of the pit; and we heard in that valley a continual howling and yelling, like people in unspeakable misery, bound in affliction and irons; and over that valley hang the discouraging clouds of confusion. Death always spreads his wings over it. In a word, it is dreadful in every way.

CHRISTIAN: From what you have said, I believe this is my way to the desired haven.

MEN: It may be your way; we will certainly not choose it for ours.

So they parted, and Christian went on his way, but with his sword drawn, in case he should be assaulted.

I saw in my dream that there was a very deep ditch on the right, running the entire length of the valley; it is that ditch into which the blind have led the blind in every age, and there both have perished miserably. On the left was a dangerous marsh; if even a good man falls into this, he can find no bottom on which to stand. It was into that bog that King David once fell and would have been smothered had not he that is able pulled him out.

The pathway here was also extremely narrow, and Christian had to be more careful than ever; for when he tried to avoid the ditch on one side, he almost slipped into the mire on the other; and when he tried to escape the mire, he had to be careful not to fall into the ditch. I heard him sigh bitterly; for, besides the dangers mentioned above, the pathway was so dark that often when he lifted up his foot to go forward, he did not know where or upon what he should set it next.

> *Poor man! Where art thou now?*
> *Thy day is night.*
> *Good man, be not cast down, thou yet art right,*
> *Thy way to heaven lies by the gates of hell;*
> *Cheer up, hold out, with thee it shall go well.*

Midway through this valley I noticed the mouth of hell close to the pathway. "Now," thought Christian, "what shall I do?" Flame and smoke spewed out continually and in such abundance, with sparks and hideous noises (things that could not be dealt with by Christian's sword, as was Apollyon), that he was forced to sheath his sword and take up another weapon, called all-prayer. So he cried, "O Lord, I beg you, deliver my soul!" Thus he went on a great while, yet still the flames reached toward him. Also he heard sorrowful voices, and sounds of great movement back and forth, so that sometimes he thought he should be torn in pieces or trodden down like mud in the streets. He saw and heard these frightful sights and dreadful noises for several miles; and reaching a place where he thought he heard a company of fiends coming forward to meet him, he stopped and began to consider what would be the best thing to do. Sometimes he had half a mind to go back; then again he thought he might be halfway through the valley, and he remembered how he had already conquered many dangers, and that the danger of going back might be much worse than going forward; so he resolved to go on. Yet the fiends seemed to be coming straight at him, and he cried out forcefully, "I will walk in the strength of the Lord God!" So the fiends gave way and came no further.

One thing I could not help noticing: by now poor Christian was so confused that he did not know his own voice. I realized this because just as he came up to the mouth of the burning pit, one of the wicked ones got behind him, and stepped up softly and whisperingly suggested terrible blasphemies to him, which he actually thought had come from his own mind. This was a greater trial to Christian than anything he had met with so far, even to think that he should now blaspheme him that he loved so much before; yet if he could have helped it, he would not have done it; but he had not the understanding to either cover his ears or to know where these blasphemies came from.

When Christian had traveled in this disconsolate condition for some considerable time, he thought he heard the voice of a man, going before him, saying, "Though I walk through the Valley of the Shadow of Death, I will fear no evil, for thou art with me."

Then he was glad, and for these reasons:

First, because he gathered from this that he was not alone in this valley. There were others here who feared God as well.

Second, since he perceived that God was with them in this dark and dismal state, then why not with him, even though in the present circumstances it did not seem so.

Third, because he hoped he could overtake them and have company by and by. So he went on and called to the man who was ahead of him; but the man did not know what to answer, for he also thought he was alone. And before long it was daybreak, and Christian said, "He has turned the shadow of death into the morning."

Now he looked back, not out of any desire to return, but to see by the light of day what hazards he had gone through in the dark. So he saw more perfectly the ditch that was on the right and the marsh that was on the left, and how narrow the path was between them; also he now saw the hobgoblins and satyrs and dragons of the pit afar off (for after daybreak they did not come near him), yet they were revealed to him according to that which is written, "He discovereth deep things out of darkness, and bringeth out to light the shadow of death."

Christian was greatly affected by his deliverance from all the dangers of his solitary way; which, though he had feared them more before, he now saw more clearly because the light of day made them conspicuous to him. And about this time the sun was rising, and this was another mercy to Christian; for you must note that though the first part of the Valley of the Shadow of Death was dangerous, this second part, which he had yet to travel, was far more dangerous. From the place where he now stood to the end of the valley, the way was filled with snares, traps, gins, nets, pits, deep holes, and slopes; had it now been dark, as it was when he came the first part of the way, and had he had a thousand souls, they would have had reason to be cast away. But as I said, the sun was rising, so he said, "His candle shineth on my head, and by his light I go through darkness."

In this light, therefore, he came to the end of the valley. And I saw in my dream that at the end of this valley lay blood, bones, ashes, and mangled bodies of pilgrims who had gone this way before; and while I was wondering about the reason for this, I saw a little ways in front of me a cave, where two giants, Pope and Pagan, had lived, by whose power and tyranny the men whose remains lay there were cruelly put to death. But Christian passed this place without much danger, which I wondered about; I have learned since that Pagan has been dead for some time, and the other, though still alive, has grown so crazy and stiff in his joints because of his age and the many dangerous skirmishes he met with in his younger days that he can now do little more than sit in the mouth of his cave, grinning at pilgrims as they go by and biting his nails because he cannot attack them.

So Christian went on his way. Yet at the sight of the Old Man who sat in the mouth of the cave, he did not know what to think, especially since the man spoke to him, saying, "You will never change till more of you be burned." But Christian kept quiet and looked cheerful and thus went by without being harmed. Then he sang:

> *O world of wonders! (I can say no less)*
> *That I should be preserved in that distress*
> *That I have met with here! O blessed be*
> *That hand that from it hath delivered me!*
> *Dangers in darkness, devils, hell, and sin*
> *Did compass me, while I this vale was in:*
> *Yea, snares and pits and traps and nets did lie*
> *My path about, that worthless, silly I*
> *Might have been catched, entangled, and cast down;*
> *But since I live, let Jesus wear the crown.*

Now as Christian went on his way, he came to a little hill, which was set there so that pilgrims might see what lay before them. Christian climbed this and, looking ahead, saw Faithful before him upon his journey. Then said Christian aloud, "Ho! Ho! So-ho! Wait, and I will be your companion." At that Faithful looked behind him, and Christian cried again, "Wait, wait until I catch up with you." But Faithful answered, "No, my life depends on it, for the avenger of blood is behind me."

At this, Christian was somewhat moved, and using all his strength, he quickly caught up with Faithful and overtook him, so that the last was first. Then Christian smiled proudly because he had gotten ahead of his brother; but not watching his feet carefully, he suddenly stumbled and fell and could not get up again until Faithful came to help him.

Then I saw in my dream that they went lovingly on together and had pleasant conversation about all the things that had happened to them on their pilgrimage; and thus Christian began:

CHRISTIAN: My honored and well-beloved brother Faithful, I am glad I have caught up with you and that God has so tempered our spirits that we can walk as companions in this pleasant path.

FAITHFUL: I had thought, dear friend, that I would have your company all the way from our town; but you started before me, so I was forced to come this far alone.

CHRISTIAN: How long did you stay in the City of Destruction before you set out after me on your pilgrimage?

FAITHFUL: Till I could stay no longer; for there was much talk after you were gone that our city would shortly be burned to the ground with fire from heaven.

CHRISTIAN: What! Did your neighbors talk like that?

FAITHFUL: Yes, for a while it was on everybody's tongue.

CHRISTIAN: What! And did no one but you leave to escape the danger?

FAITHFUL: Though there was, as I said, much talk about it, I do not think they really believed it. For in the heat of conversation I heard some of them speak contemptuously of you and your desperate journey (for that's what they called this pilgrimage of yours). But I did believe, and still do, that the end of our city will be with fire and brimstone from above; and therefore I have made my escape.

CHRISTIAN: Did you hear any talk of neighbor Pliable?

FAITHFUL: Yes, Christian, I heard that he followed you till he came to the Swamp of Despond, where, as some said, he fell in. He did not want it known that he had done so, but I am sure he was covered with that kind of dirt.

CHRISTIAN: And what did the neighbors say to him?

FAITHFUL: Since his return he has been greatly ridiculed by all sorts of people; some mock and despise him and scarcely anyone will give him work. He is now seven times worse than if he had never left the city.

CHRISTIAN: But why should they be so set against him, since they also despise the way that he forsook?

FAITHFUL: They say hang him, he is a traitor! He was not true to his profession. I think God has stirred up even his enemies to scoff at him because he has forsaken the way.

CHRISTIAN: Did you talk with him before you left?

FAITHFUL: I met him once in the streets, but he crossed over to the other side, as though ashamed of what he had done. So I didn't speak to him.

CHRISTIAN: Well, when I first set out I had great hopes for that man; but now I fear he will perish in the overthrow of the city, for he is like the true proverb: "The dog is turned to his own vomit again, and the sow that was washed to her wallowing in the mire."

FAITHFUL: Those are my fears for him too, but who can prevent the inevitable?

CHRISTIAN: Well, neighbor Faithful, let us leave him and talk of things that more immediately concern us. Tell me about your experiences on the way, for I know you have encountered some things, or else it will go down as a miracle.

FAITHFUL: I escaped the Swamp that you fell into and got up to the gate without that danger; only I met with one whose name was Wanton, who would like to have done me harm.

CHRISTIAN: It was well you escaped her net. Joseph was tempted by her, and he escaped her as you did; but it almost cost him his life. What did she do to you?

FAITHFUL: You cannot imagine unless you know what a flattering tongue she has. She made every effort to get me to turn aside with her, promising me all kinds of satisfaction.

CHRISTIAN: I bet she did not promise you the satisfaction of a good conscience.

FAITHFUL: You know what I mean; all kinds of carnal and fleshly satisfaction.

CHRISTIAN: Thank God you have escaped her, for the "abhorred of the Lord shall fall" into her trap.

FAITHFUL: Well, I don't know whether I completely escaped her or not.

CHRISTIAN: Why, I trust you did not consent to her desires?

FAITHFUL: No, not to defile myself; for I remembered an old writing that I had seen, which said, "Her steps lead straight to hell." So I shut my eyes so I would not be bewitched by her looks. Then she spoke harshly to me, and I went my way.

CHRISTIAN: Did you meet with any other assault as you traveled?

FAITHFUL: When I came to the foot of the hill called Difficulty, I met a very aged man who asked me who I was and where I was going. I told him that I was a pilgrim going to the Celestial City. Then he said, "You look like an honest fellow; would you be content to live with me for the wages I shall give you?" Then I asked him his name and where he lived. He said his name was the First Adam and that he lived in the town of Deceit. I asked him then what kind of work he had and what wages he would pay. He told me that his work contained many delights and for my wages I should be his heir. I asked him what kind of house he had and what other servants. So he told me that his house contained all the delicious things in the world and that his servants were his children. Then I asked how many children he had. He said he had but three daughters: The Lust of the Flesh, The Lust of the Eyes, and The Pride of Life, and that I should marry them all if I wanted. Then I asked how long he would want me to live with him, and he told me, as long as he lived himself.

CHRISTIAN: Well, what conclusion did you and the old man come to at last?

FAITHFUL: Why, at first I was somewhat inclined to go with the man, for I thought he spoke fairly; but looking at his forehead as I talked with him, I saw written, "Put off the old man with his deeds."

CHRISTIAN: And what then?

FAITHFUL: Then it came burning hot into my mind that whatever he said and however he flattered, when he got me home to his house, he would sell me as a slave. So I told him he could quit talking, for I would not come near the door of his house. Then he reviled me and told me he would send one after me who would make my way miserable. So I turned to leave him; but just as I turned, I felt him take hold of my flesh and give me such a deadly jerk backward that I thought he had pulled part of me after himself. This made me cry, "O wretched man!" and I went on my way up the hill.

Now when I had gotten about halfway up, I looked behind and saw someone coming after me swift as the wind; he overtook me just about where the shelter stands.

CHRISTIAN: Just there did I sit down to rest; but being overcome with sleep, I lost this scroll out of my coat.

FAITHFUL: Wait, good brother, hear me out. As soon as the man overtook me, he knocked me down and I lay there like I was dead. When I came to myself again, I asked him why he had treated me so. He said, "Because of your secret interest in the First Adam." And with that he struck me another deadly blow on the breast and beat me down backward so that I lay at his feet as before. So when I came to myself again, I cried to him, "Have mercy!" But he said, "I don't know how to show mercy," and with that knocked me down again. No doubt he would have killed me, if someone had not come by and told him to stop.

CHRISTIAN: Who told him to stop?

FAITHFUL: I did not know him at first, but as he went by I saw the holes in his hands and his side; then I concluded that he was our Lord. So I went up the hill.

CHRISTIAN: That man who overtook you was Moses. He spares no one, nor does he know how to show mercy to those who break his law.

FAITHFUL: I know it very well; it was not the first time he has met with me. It was he who came to me when I lived securely at home and told me he would burn my house over my head if I stayed there.

CHRISTIAN: But didn't you see the house that stood there on the top of the hill on the side where Moses met you?

FAITHFUL: Yes, and the lions too, before I came to it: but I think the lions were asleep. And because there was so much daylight left, I passed by the porter and came down the hill.

CHRISTIAN: He told me that he saw you go by, but I wish you had stopped at the house, for they would have showed you so many wonderful things that you would never forget. But tell me, did you meet anyone in the Valley of Humility?

FAITHFUL: Yes, I met with Discontent, who tried to persuade me to go back with him; his reason for doing so was that the valley was totally without honor. He told me that to go there was to disobey friends like Pride, Arrogance, Self-conceit, Worldly-glory, and others, who would be offended if I made a fool of myself by wading through this valley.

CHRISTIAN: How did you answer him?

FAITHFUL: I told him that although all these that he named might claim kinship with me—and rightly so, for they were my relatives in the flesh—yet since I became a pilgrim they have disowned me, just as I have rejected them; and therefore it is as though they had never been in my family. I also told him that he had quite misrepresented this valley, for "before honor is humility, and a haughty spirit before a fall." Therefore, said I, I would rather go through this valley to the honor accounted so by the wisest, than choose that which he considered worthy of our affections.

CHRISTIAN: Did you meet with anything else in that valley?

FAITHFUL: Yes, I met with Shame; but of all those I encountered on my pilgrimage, he, I think, bears the wrong name, for he is without shame.

CHRISTIAN: Why? What did he say to you?

FAITHFUL: Why he objected to religion itself, saying it was a pitiful, low, sneaking business for a man to care about religion; he said that a tender conscience was an unmanly thing and that a man who watches his words and ways loses the freedom that is rightfully his in this age and makes him look ridiculous. He also objected to religion on the grounds that few mighty, rich, or wise people care about it; they are not foolish enough to risk losing everything for the unknown. He said that most of those who were pilgrims were poor and uneducated. Yes, he went on at this rate about a great many more things: that it was a shame to sit whining and mourning under a sermon, and a shame to come sighing and groaning home; that it was a shame to ask my neighbor's forgiveness for petty faults or to make restitution. He said also that religion made a man seem odd to great people because of its objection to a few vices, which he called by more dignified names, and made a man respect the lower classes because they were in the same religious fraternity. And wasn't this, said he, a shame?

CHRISTIAN: And what did you say to him?

FAITHFUL: Say! I didn't know what to say at first. He kept at me so that my face became red. But at last I began to think about the fact that "that which is highly esteemed among men is abomination in God's sight." And I thought, this Shame tells me what men are, but he tells me nothing about what God or the Word of God is. And then I thought, at the day of judgment we shall not be awarded death or life according to the bullying spirits of this world, but according to the wisdom and law of the Highest. Therefore, thought I, what God says is best, though all the men in the world are against it. Seeing, then, that God prefers a tender conscience; seeing that they who make themselves fools for the kingdom of heaven are wisest; and seeing that the poor man who loves Christ is richer than the greatest man in the world that hates him, I said, Shame, depart! You are an enemy to my salvation! If I listen to you instead of my sovereign Lord, how can I look him in the face when he returns? If I am ashamed of his ways and servants now, how can I expect his blessing?

But this Shame was a bold villain; I could hardly get rid of him. He kept following me and whispering in my ear about the various things that are wrong with religion. But at last I told him it was futile for him to continue this business; for those things that he disdained, I valued the most. So finally I got past this troublesome one, and when I had gotten rid of him, I began to sing:

The trials that those men do meet withal,
That are obedient to the heavenly call,
Are manifold, and suited to the flesh,
And come, and come, and come again afresh;
That now, or sometimes else, we by them may
Be taken, overcome, and cast away.
Oh, let the pilgrims, let the pilgrims then
Be vigilant, and quit themselves like men.

CHRISTIAN: I am glad, my brother, that you withstood this villain so bravely; for as you have said, I think he has the wrong name. He boldly follows us in the streets and attempts to put us to shame before all men: that is, to make us ashamed of that which is good. But if he was not himself without shame, he would never try to do what he does. But let us still resist him; for despite all his bragging, he only furthers the cause of fools. "The wise shall inherit glory," said Solomon, "but shame shall be the promotion of fools."

FAITHFUL: For help against Shame, I think we must cry to him who would have us be valiant for truth upon the earth.

CHRISTIAN: You speak the truth. But, tell me, did you meet anyone else in that valley?

FAITHFUL: No, I did not, for I had sunshine all the rest of the way through it, and also through the Valley of the Shadow of Death.

CHRISTIAN: You fared better than I did then. Almost as soon as I entered into that valley, I began a long and dreadful battle with that foul fiend Apollyon; in fact, I thought he was going to kill me, especially when he got me down and crushed me to pieces; for as he threw me, my sword flew out of my hand; he even told me that he had me. But I cried to God, and he heard me and delivered me out of all my troubles. Then I entered into the Valley of the Shadow of Death and had no light for almost half the way through it. Over and over I thought I was going to be killed there, but at last day broke and the sun rose, and I went the rest of the way with far more ease and quiet.

Moreover, I saw in my dream that as they went on, Faithful happened to look to one side and saw a man whose name is Talkative walking beside them but at some distance away (for here it was wide enough for them all to walk side by side). He was a tall man and more handsome at a distance than up close. To this man Faithful addressed himself in this manner:

FAITHFUL: Friend, where are you going? To the heavenly country?

TALKATIVE: I am going to that place.

FAITHFUL: Good. Then I hope we may have your company.

TALKATIVE: I will gladly be your companion.

FAITHFUL: Come on then, and let us travel together and spend our time discussing things that are profitable.

TALKATIVE: I enjoy talking about worthwhile matters, and I am glad that I have met with those who are inclined the same way; for to tell you the truth, there are only a few who care to spend their time in this manner as they travel; most choose instead to argue about things that don't matter, and that troubles me.

FAITHFUL: That is indeed regretful, for what is more worthy of the use of the tongue and mouth of men on earth than the things of the God of heaven?

TALKATIVE: I like you, for your words are full of conviction. And I will add, what is more pleasant or more profitable than to talk about the things of God? (That is, if a man takes any delight in things that are wonderful.) For instance, if a man enjoys talking about the history or the mystery of things, or if a man loves to talk about miracles, wonders, or signs, where will he find anything more wonderful than that which is recorded in the Holy Scripture?

FAITHFUL: That is true. But our intention should be to profit from such things in our conversation.

TALKATIVE: That is just what I said. For to talk of such things is most profitable; and by doing so, a man may gain knowledge of many things, such as the vanity of earthly things and the benefit of things above. But more particularly, by this a man may learn the necessity of the new birth, the insufficiency of our works, the need of Christ's righteousness, and so forth. By talking, a man may learn what it is to repent, to believe, to pray, to suffer, or the like; he may also learn the great promises and consolations of the gospel, to his own comfort. Further, by this a man may learn to refute false opinions, to confirm the truth, and to instruct the ignorant.

FAITHFUL: I am glad to hear these things from you.

TALKATIVE: Sadly, the lack of such talk is why so few understand the need for faith and the necessity of a work of grace in their soul in order to obtain eternal life; instead, they ignorantly live by the works of the law, which cannot lead a man to the kingdom of heaven.

FAITHFUL: But heavenly knowledge of these matters is the gift of God; no man can attain these things by human means, or only by talking about them.

TALKATIVE: All this I know very well. For a man can receive nothing unless it is given him from heaven; all is of grace, not of works. I could give you a hundred scriptures that confirm this.

FAITHFUL: Well then, what shall we talk about?

TALKATIVE: Whatever you want. I will talk of things heavenly or things earthly; things moral or things evangelical; things sacred or things profane; things past or things to come; things foreign or things at home; things essential or things circumstantial; provided that all this is done to our profit.

Now Faithful began to marvel at what he heard. And stepping to Christian—who had been walking all this time by himself—he said softly, "What a brave companion we have! Surely this man will make an excellent pilgrim."

At this, Christian smiled a little and said, "This man with whom you are so taken could, with his tongue, deceive twenty who don't know him."

FAITHFUL: Do you know him then?

CHRISTIAN: Know him! Yes, better than he knows himself.

FAITHFUL: Who is he?

CHRISTIAN: His name is Talkative, and he lives in our town. I'm surprised that you don't know him, but our town is large.

FAITHFUL: Whose son is he? And where does he live?

CHRISTIAN: He is the son of Say-well and lives in Prating Row; all who are acquainted with him know him by the name of Talkative. And despite his fine tongue, he is a contemptible fellow.

FAITHFUL: Well, he seems to be a very handsome man.

CHRISTIAN: He seems so to those who are not thoroughly acquainted with him; for he is best abroad; near home he is ugly. Your saying that he is a handsome man brings to mind what I have observed in the work of artists, whose paintings look best at a distance, while up close they are unpleasing.

FAITHFUL: I think you are joking with me.

CHRISTIAN: God forbid that I should jest about such a matter, or that I should accuse anyone falsely! I will tell you more about him. This man enjoys any company and any talk; as he talks with you now, so will he talk when he is in the tavern; and the more he drinks, the more he talks; religion has no place in his heart, or his home, or his behavior; he is all talk, and his religion is his tongue.

FAITHFUL: You don't say! Then I have been greatly deceived by this man.

CHRISTIAN: Deceived! You may be sure of it. Remember the proverb, "They say and do not"; but "the kingdom of God is not in word, but in power." He talks of prayer, of repentance, of faith, and of the new birth; but he only talks of them. I have been with his family and have observed him both at home and abroad; and I know that what I say of him is the truth. His house is as empty of religion as the white of an egg is of flavor. There is neither prayer there, nor sign of repentance for sin; even the animals serve God far better than he. For those who know him, he brings shame and reproach to the name of the Lord; in that end of the town where he lives, he gives religion a bad name. The folks who know him say, "He's a saint abroad and a devil at home." Certainly his poor family finds it so; he is rude and abusive and so unreasonable with his servants that they never know how to approach him. Men that have any dealings with him say it is better to deal with a Turk than with him; for they will receive fairer treatment at their hands. This Talkative, if it is possible, will outdo them in defrauding, deceiving, and getting the better of others by unscrupulous means. Besides, he brings up his sons to act the same way; and if he finds in any of them a foolish timidness (for that is what he calls a tender conscience), he calls them fools and blockheads and will not employ them or recommend them to others. I believe that his wicked life has caused many to stumble and fall and that he will, if God does not prevent it, cause the ruin of many more.

FAITHFUL: Well, my brother, I have to believe you; not only because you say you know him, but also because you look at men as a Christian. Also, I do not believe you say these things out of malice, but because they are true.

CHRISTIAN: Had I known him no better than you do, I probably would have thought the same of him as you did at first; and had I heard these things about him only from those who are enemies of religion, I would have thought it slander—something that often falls from bad men's mouths about good men's names and professions—but from my own knowledge, I can prove he is guilty of all these things and more. Besides, good men are ashamed of him;

they can neither call him brother nor friend; the very sound of his name makes them blush, if they know him.

FAITHFUL: Well, I see that saying and doing are two different things, and from here on I shall be careful to observe this distinction.

CHRISTIAN: They are two different things indeed, and are as diverse as the soul and the body; for as the body without the soul is but a dead carcass, so are words without deeds. The soul of religion is the practical part: "Pure religion and undefiled, before God and the Father, is this, To visit the fatherless and widows in their affliction, and to keep himself unspotted from the world." This, Talkative is not aware of; he thinks that hearing and saying will make a good Christian, and thus he deceives his own soul. Hearing is but the sowing of the seed; talking does not prove that the heart and life are fruitful; and let us rest assured that at the day of judgment, men shall be judged according to their fruits. It will not be said then, "Did you believe?" but, "Were you doers or talkers only?" and they shall be judged accordingly. The end of the world can be compared to our harvest; and you know that at harvest men are interested in nothing but the fruit. Not that anything can be accepted that is not the result of faith, but I say this to show you how insignificant the profession of Talkative will be at that time.

FAITHFUL: This brings to mind the words of Moses, when he described the beast that is clean. It is one that has a split hoof and chews the cud; not one that only has a split hoof, or one that only chews the cud. The rabbit chews the cud, but is unclean because he does not have a split hoof. And this is what Talkative resembles: he seeks knowledge by chewing upon the word, but he does not split from his sinful ways; so, like the rabbit, he is unclean.

CHRISTIAN: For all I know you have spoken the true gospel sense of those texts. And I will add another thing. Paul calls some men, and those great talkers too, "sounding brass and tinkling cymbals"; that is, as he expounds in another place, "things without life, giving sound." Things without life are those things without the true faith and grace of the gospel; and consequently, such things shall never enter the kingdom of heaven among those who are the children of life; even though they sound, by their talk, as if they were the tongue or voice of an angel.

FAITHFUL: Well, I was not overly fond of his company before, but now I am truly sick of it. How can we get rid of him?

CHRISTIAN: Take my advice and do as I tell you and you will find that he will soon be sick of your company too, unless God touches his heart and turns it.

FAITHFUL: What would you have me do?

CHRISTIAN: Go to him and enter into some serious discussion about the power of religion; and when he has agreed with you, for he will, then ask him point-blank whether this power has been established in his heart, house, or behavior.

Faithful stepped forward again and said to Talkative, "How are you doing?"

TALKATIVE: Well, thank you. I thought we would have talked a great deal by this time.

FAITHFUL: Well, if you will, we will go to it now; and since you left it with me to state the question, let it be this: How can you tell when the saving grace of God is in the heart of man?

TALKATIVE: I see that our talk must be about the power of things. Well, it is a very good question, and I am willing to answer you. First, and in brief, when the grace of God is in the heart, it cries out against sin. Second—

FAITHFUL: Wait! Hold on! Let's consider one thing at a time. I think you should say instead that grace evidences itself by causing the soul to abhor its own sin.

TALKATIVE: Why, what difference is there between crying out against and abhorring sin?

FAITHFUL: Oh, a great deal. A man may cry out against sin, as a general policy, but he cannot abhor it unless he has a godly hatred of it. I have heard many cry out against sin in the pulpit, who still live with it in the heart, home, and behavior. Joseph's master's wife cried out with a loud voice, as though she were very holy; but she would willingly have committed adultery with him. Some cry out against sin even as the mother playfully cries out against her child in her lap, calling her a naughty girl, and then begins hugging and kissing her.

TALKATIVE: You lie in wait to catch me, I see.

FAITHFUL: No, I just want to set things straight. Now what is the second thing by which you would prove the existence of a work of grace in the heart?

TALKATIVE: Great knowledge of gospel mysteries.

FAITHFUL: This sign should have been first; but first or last, it is also false; for knowledge, great knowledge, of the mysteries of the gospel may be obtained, and yet there may be no work of grace in the soul. Yes, a man may have all knowledge and still not be a child of God. Christ said, "Do you know all these things?" and the disciples answered, "Yes." Then he added, "Blessed are you if you do them." The blessing is not in the knowing, but in the doing. For knowledge is not always accompanied by actions, like the servant who knows what his master wants but does not do it. A man may have the knowledge of angels and still not be a Christian; therefore your sign is not true. Indeed, to know is a thing that pleases talkers and boasters; but to do is that which pleases God. Not that the heart can be good without knowledge; for without that, the heart is nothing. There is knowledge and there is knowledge: knowledge that knows about things; and knowledge that is accompanied with the grace of faith and love, which causes a man to do the will of God from the heart. The first of these will satisfy the talker; but the true Christian is not content without the other. "Give me understanding, and I shall keep thy law; yea, I shall observe it with my whole heart."

TALKATIVE: You are trying to trip me up again. This is not edifying.

FAITHFUL: Well, if you please, give me another sign of this work of grace for our discussion.

TALKATIVE: No, for I see we shall not agree.

FAITHFUL: If you will not, then will you let me do so?

TALKATIVE: Feel free to do so.

FAITHFUL: A work of grace in the soul is evident both to him who has it and to those standing by. The one who has it is convicted of sin, especially of the defilement of his nature and the sin of unbelief (for which he is sure to be damned if he does not find mercy at God's hand by faith in Jesus Christ). This conviction causes him sorrow and shame for his sin; moreover, it reveals to him his need to make himself right with the Savior of the world, which makes him hunger and thirst for God; and it is this hungering and thirsting for salvation that God has promised to satisfy. Now, his joy and peace are equivalent to the strength or weakness of his faith in his Savior, as are his love of holiness and his desire to know more of the Savior and serve him in this world. But though it evidences itself to him in this way, seldom is he able to conclude that this is a work of grace, because his corruption and his abused reason make him mis-judge this matter; therefore a very sound judgment is required before he can conclude with assurance that this is a work of grace.

To others, it is evident in other ways:

1. By an experiential confession of his faith in Christ.

2. By a life that answers to that confession; that is, a life of holiness—holiness of heart, holiness of family (if he has a

family), and holiness of behavior in the world. Such holiness teaches him to abhor his own sin, and this he does in private; to suppress sin in his family; and to promote holiness in the world—not only in words, as a hypocrite or talkative person may do, but in a practical subjection, in faith and love, to the power of the Word. And now, sir, as to this brief description of the work of grace and the evidence of it, if you have any objection, object; if not, then may I raise a second question?

TALKATIVE: No, it is not for me to object, but to listen. So give me your second question.

FAITHFUL: It is this: Do you experience the first part of this description of the work of grace? And do your life and behavior testify to this? Or is your religion in word or in tongue, and not in deed and truth? And if you do desire to answer me in this, say no more than you know the God above will say "Amen" to and only that which your conscience can justify; "For it is not the one who commends himself who is approved, but the one whom the Lord commends." Besides, it is very wicked to say "I am thus and thus" when my behavior and all my neighbors tell me I lie.

At first Talkative began to blush; but then regaining his poise, he replied thus:

TALKATIVE: You come now to experience, conscience, and God, and to appeal to him to judge what is said. This kind of discussion I did not expect; nor am I disposed to answer such questions, because I do not consider myself bound to do so, unless you are assuming the role of a catechizer; and even if you did that, I might still refuse to make you my judge. But tell me, will you, why you ask me such questions?

FAITHFUL: Because I saw you were eager to talk. Besides, to tell you the truth, I have heard that you are a man whose religion is all talk and that your behavior says that what you profess with your mouth is a lie. They say you bring disgrace to the people of God and that religion fares the worse because of your ungodly behavior; they say that some have already stumbled because of your wicked ways and that more are in danger of being destroyed by them; your religion and the tavern and covetousness and uncleanness and swearing and lying and bad company will be judged together. There is a proverb, said of a whore: that she is a shame to all women. So are you a shame to all professing Christians.

TALKATIVE: Since you are ready to listen to reports and to judge so rashly, I can only conclude that you are an ill-tempered man who is not fit to converse with. Farewell.

Then Christian came up and said to his brother, "I told you what would happen: your words and his lusts could not agree; he would rather leave your company than change his life. But he is gone, and I say, let him go; it is his loss. He has saved us the trouble of leaving him; as he is, he would have been a hindrance to us. Besides, the apostle says, 'From such withdraw thyself.'"

FAITHFUL: I am glad we had this little discussion with him, though, for perhaps he will think of it again sometime. However, I have been forthright with him, and so I am innocent of his blood if he perishes.

CHRISTIAN: You did well to talk as plainly to him as you did; there is little of this faithful dealing with men nowadays, and that makes religion distasteful to many; for such talkative fools whose religion is only in word, and whose behavior is corrupt (yet being often admitted into the fellowship of the godly), do puzzle the world, blemish Christianity, and grieve the sincere. I wish that all men would deal with them as you have done. Then they would either be made more conformable to religion or the company of saints would be too hot for them.

Then Faithful said:

> *How Talkative at first lifts up his plumes!*
> *How bravely doth he speak! How he presumes*
> *To drive down all before him! But so soon*
> *As Faithful talks of heart-work, like the moon*
> *That's past the full, into the wane he goes.*
> *And so will all, but he that heart-work knows.*

Thus they went on talking of what they had seen on the way, and so made that part of the journey easy, which would otherwise, no doubt, have been tedious, for now they went through a wilderness.

When they were almost out of this wilderness, Faithful happened to look back and spied someone coming after them, and he recognized him. "Oh!" said Faithful, "Look who comes yonder!" Then Christian looked and said, "It is my good friend Evangelist." "And my good friend too," said Faithful, "for it was he who told me the way to the gate." Now Evangelist had caught up with them and greeted them:

EVANGELIST: Peace be with you, dearly beloved, and peace be with those who have helped you.

CHRISTIAN: Welcome, welcome, my good Evangelist! The sight of your face reminds me of your former kindness and your work for my eternal good.

FAITHFUL: A thousand times welcome! Your company, O sweet Evangelist, how desirable it is to us poor pilgrims!

EVANGELIST: How have you fared, my friends, since I saw you last? What have you met with, and how have you behaved yourselves?

Then Christian and Faithful told him of all the things that had happened to them along the way, and how, and with what difficulty, they had arrived at that place.

EVANGELIST: I am glad, not that you have met with trials, but that you have been victors and that you have, despite many weaknesses, continued in the way to this very day.

I say, I am glad of this, and that for my own sake as well as yours. I have sowed, and you have reaped; and the day is coming when both he that sowed and they that reaped shall rejoice together; that is, if you hold out, for in due time you shall reap, if you faint not. The crown is before you, and it is an incorruptible one; so run that you may obtain it. Some set out for this crown, and after they have gone far for it, another comes in and takes it from them; hold on to what you have, and let no man take your crown. You are not yet out of the devil's range; you have not resisted with your own blood; let the kingdom be always before you, and believe steadfastly in those things that are invisible. Let nothing that is on this side of the other world become a part of you; and above all, watch out for the lusts of your own hearts, for they are deceitful and desperately wicked; endure with determination, for you have all the power in heaven and earth on your side.

Christian thanked him for his exhortation and told him they would like him to speak further for their help the rest of the way, for they knew he was a prophet and could tell them of things that might happen to them and how they might resist and overcome those things. Faithful seconded this request.

EVANGELIST: My sons, you have heard in the words of the gospel that you must pass through many tribulations to enter into the kingdom of heaven. And, again, that in every city you face prison and hardship; and therefore you cannot expect to go long on your pilgrimage without them, in one form or other. You have already found some of the truth of these testimonies, and more will immediately follow; for now, as you see, you are almost out of this wilderness, and therefore before long you will enter a town that you will soon see before you; and in that town you will be harshly attacked by enemies who will try to kill you; and you may be sure that one or both of you must seal your testimony with blood; but be faithful unto death, and the King will give you a crown of life. He who shall die there, although his death will be unnatural and his pain perhaps great, will have the better of his fellow—not only because he will arrive at the Celestial City sooner, but because he will escape many miseries that the other will meet with on the rest of his journey. But when you have come to the town and have found fulfilled what I have told you, then remember your friend; behave like men and commit yourselves to your faithful Creator and continue to do good.

Then I saw in my dream that when Christian and Faithful had emerged from the wilderness, they soon saw a town ahead of them, and the name of that town was Vanity; and at the town there was a fair, called Vanity Fair, which went on all the year long. It was named Vanity Fair because all that was sold there was vain or worthless, and all who came there were vain. As the wise saying goes, "all that cometh is vanity."

This fair was no newly established business, but a thing of long-standing. I will show you how it originally began.

Almost five thousand years ago there were pilgrims walking to the Celestial City, as these two honest persons were; and Beelzebub, Apollyon, and Legion, with their companions, seeing that the pilgrims always passed through this town of Vanity, decided to set up a fair here that would last all year long, where they would sell all sorts of vanity: houses, lands, trades, places, honors, promotions, titles, countries, kingdoms, lusts, pleasures, and delights of all sorts, such as prostitutes, wives, husbands, children, masters, servants, lives, blood, bodies, souls, silver, gold, pearls, and precious stones.

At this fair one could always see jugglers, cheats, games, plays, fools, mimics, tricksters, and scoundrels of every kind. Here one also could see, without charge, thefts, murders, adulteries, liars, and things of scarlet.

And as in other fairs of less importance where there are several rows and streets with proper names where wares are sold, so here you had rows and streets (namely, countries and kingdoms) where the wares of this fair could be found. Here was the Britain Row, the French Row, the Italian Row, the Spanish Row, the German Row, where several sorts of vanities were sold. But just as one commodity is the most popular at other fairs, so it was in this fair, for here Rome and her merchandise were greatly promoted; only our English nation and a few others have taken a dislike to it.

Now, as I said, the path to the Celestial City passed right through this town where this fair was kept; and if anyone wanted to go to the city and yet not go through this town, he must "leave this world." The Prince of princes himself, when he was here, passed through this town, and that was on a fair day too; and I believe it was Beelzebub, the chief lord of this fair, who invited him to buy some of his vanities; yes, he said he would make him lord of the fair if he would only worship him as he went through the town. And Beelzebub took him from street to street and showed him all the kingdoms of the world so that he might, if possible, allure the Blessed One to lower himself and buy some of his vanities; but the Blessed One was not interested in the merchandise and left the town without spending one cent on these vanities.

This fair, therefore, was an ancient thing, of long-standing, and a very large fair; and these pilgrims, as I said, had to pass through it. But when they entered the fair, all the people got excited, and the town was soon in an uproar around them. There were several reasons for this:

First, the pilgrims' clothing was different from any worn by those who were trading at the fair. Therefore, the people stared at them rudely: some said they were fools, some said they were madmen, and some said they were outlandish.

Second, just as they had doubts about their apparel, so they were uncertain of their speech, for few could understand what they said. Christian and Faithful spoke the language of Canaan, but those who ran the fair were the men of this world; so from one end of the fair to the other they seemed like barbarians to each other.

Third, and this greatly amused the merchants, these pilgrims were not interested in any of their wares; they didn't even want to look at them; and if they called upon them to buy, they would put their fingers in their ears and cry, "Turn away mine eyes from beholding vanity," and look upward, signifying that their business was in heaven.

One, noticing the conduct of the men, said to them mockingly, "What would you buy?" They looked at him gravely and answered, "We buy the truth." This gave them even more reason to despise the men; some mocked them, some reproached them, and some called upon others to attack them. At last this caused a great commotion in the fair, so much so that there was total disorder. Presently word was brought to the governor of the fair, who quickly came down and deputized some of his most trusted friends to take these two men into custody and question them. So the men were brought to trial, and those who examined them asked where they came from, where they were going, and why they were wearing such unusual clothing. The men told them that they were pilgrims and strangers in the world, that they were going to their own country, which was the heavenly Jerusalem, and that they had given the men of the town and the merchants no reason to abuse them or hinder their journey, except that when one asked them what they would buy, they said they would buy the truth. But those who had been appointed to examine them believed them to be nothing other than madmen or those who had come to cause confusion in the fair. So they beat them and smeared them with dirt and put them into a cage to make a spectacle of them to all who were at the fair.

Behold Vanity Fair! the pilgrims there
Are chained and stoned beside;

Even so it was our Lord passed here,
And on Mount Calvary died.

There they lay for some time and were the objects of any man's sport, or malice, or revenge, while the governor of the fair laughed at all that happened to them. But because Christian and Faithful were patient and did not return evil for evil, instead giving good words for bad and kindness for injuries done, some men in the fair that were more observant and less prejudiced than the rest began to reprimand and blame the baser ones for their continual abuses to the two men; they therefore flew at them in anger, considering them as bad as the men in the cage and telling them that they seemed to be their confederates and should share their misfortunes. The others replied that for all they could see, the men were quiet and sober and intended nobody any harm, and that there were many who traded in their fair who deserved to be put into the cage more than the two men they had abused.

Thus after various words had been exchanged on both sides (during which the two men behaved wisely and soberly), they fell to fighting among themselves and injuring one another. Then these two poor men were taken to court again and charged with being guilty of causing the latest trouble in the fair. So they beat them mercilessly and led them in chains up and down the fair as an example to others, lest any should speak in their behalf or join them. But Christian and Faithful behaved even more wisely and bore the humiliation and shame with so much meekness and patience that they won several of the men in the fair to their side (though few in comparison to the rest). This made the others so enraged that they decided the two men should die for what they had done and for deluding the men of the fair.

Then they returned the men to the cage and fastened their feet in the stocks, until further orders should be given.

Here Christian and Faithful recalled what they had heard from their faithful friend Evangelist and were strengthened, for their sufferings confirmed what he had told them would happen to them. They also comforted each other that whoever was chosen to suffer should be blessed; therefore, each man secretly wished that he might have that honor; but they committed themselves to the all-wise will of the one who rules all things, content to abide in their present condition until he should will otherwise.

Finally a time was set for their trial, and they were brought before their enemies and arraigned. The judge's name was Lord Hate-good. Their indictment was the same as before, with a slight variation in form, and the basic contents stated:

"That they are enemies of and disturbers of their trade; that they have caused commotion and dissension in the town and have won a certain party to their own dangerous opinions, in contempt for the law of their prince."

Now, Faithful, play the man, speak for thy God:
Fear not the wickeds' malice; nor their rod!
Speak boldly, man, the truth is on thy side:
Die for it, and to life in triumph ride.

Then Faithful began to answer their charges, saying that he had only opposed that which had opposed him who is higher than the highest. "And as for disturbance," he said, "I make none, being myself a man of peace; the parties that were won to us were won by our truth and innocence, and they have only turned from the worse to the better. And as to the king you talk of, since he is Beelzebub, the enemy of our Lord, I defy him and all his angels."

Then it was proclaimed that those who had anything to say for their lord the king against the prisoner at the bar should appear and give their evidence. So three witnesses came in, namely, Envy,

Superstition, and Pickthank. They were then asked if they knew the prisoner at the bar, and what they had to say for their lord the king against him.

Then Envy stood up and said, "My Lord, I have known this man a long time and will attest under oath before this honorable bench that he is—"

JUDGE: Hold on a moment! Administer the oath.

So they swore him in.

Then he said, "My Lord, this man, regardless of his name, is one of the vilest men in our country. He does not respect prince or people, law or custom, but does all he can to impress others with his disloyal notions, which he calls principles of faith and holiness. And I heard him once myself affirm that Christianity and the customs of our town of Vanity were diametrically opposed and could not be reconciled. By which, my Lord, he not only condemns all our good deeds, but also us for doing them.

JUDGE: Have you any more to say?

ENVY: My Lord, I could say much more, only I don't want to weary the court. Yet if, when the other gentlemen have given their evidence, there is not enough to convict him, I will enlarge my testimony against him.

So he was told to stand by. Then they called Superstition and told him to look at the prisoner; they also asked what evidence he had for their lord the king against the man. Then they swore him in and he began.

SUPERSTITION: My Lord, I don't know this man very well, nor do I want to; however, from some conversation I had with him the other day, I do know that he is a troublemaker; for while talking with him, I heard him say that our religion was worthless and by no means pleasing to God. Your Lordship very well knows that by saying this he means that we worship in vain, that we are still in our sins, and finally shall be damned; and that is what I have to say.

Then Pickthank was sworn in and told to state what he knew in behalf of their lord the king against the prisoner at the bar.

PICKTHANK: My Lord, and gentlemen, I have known of this fellow for a long time, and have heard him say things that ought not to be said; for he has reviled our noble prince Beelzebub, and has spoken contemptuously of his honorable friends, the Lord Old Man, the Lord Carnal Delight, the Lord Luxurious, the Lord Desire of Vain-glory, my old Lord Lechery, Sir Having Greedy, along with all the rest of our nobility; and he has said, moreover, that if all men believed as he did, not one of these noblemen would dwell in this town any longer. Besides, he has not been afraid to speak against you, my Lord, who are now his judge, calling you an ungodly villain and many other vilifying terms, with which he has slandered most of the gentlemen of our town.

When Pickthank had told his tale, the judge directed his speech to the prisoner at the bar, saying, "You renegade, heretic, and traitor, have you heard what these honest gentlemen have witnessed against you?"

FAITHFUL: May I say a few words in my own defense?

JUDGE: Sir, sir, you deserve to die; yet so that all men may see our fairness to you, let us hear what you, vile renegade, have to say.

FAITHFUL: First, then, in answer to what Mr. Envy has said, I never said anything but this: That any rule, or laws, or custom, or people that are against the Word of God are diametrically opposed to Christianity. If I have spoken amiss in this, convince me of my error, and I am ready to recant before you.

As to the second, Mr. Superstition and his charge against me, I said only this: That a Divine faith is required in the worship of God; but there can be no Divine faith without a Divine revelation of the will of God. Therefore, anything that is done in the worship of God that is not in agreement with Divine revelation must be done by a human faith, which will not bring eternal life.

As to what Mr. Pickthank has said, I say (avoiding terms that would accuse me of reviling and the like) that the prince of this town and his attendants, named by this gentleman, are more fit for hell than for this town and country; and so the Lord have mercy upon me!

Then the judge called to the jury, who had been standing by, listening and observing: "Gentlemen of the jury, you see this man who has caused such a great uproar in this town. You have also heard the testimony of these worthy gentlemen against him. Also you have heard his reply and confession. You must now decide whether he is to live or die; but first I think it proper to instruct you in our law.

"There was an Act ordered in the days of Pharaoh the Great, servant to our prince, so that those of a contrary religion should not multiply and grow too strong; this provided that their males should be thrown into the river. There was also an Act carried out in the days of Nebuchadnezzar the Great, another of our prince's servants, ordering that whoever would not fall down and worship his golden image should be thrown into a fiery furnace. There was also an Act in the days of Darius that ruled that whoever, at a certain time, called upon any god but him should be cast into the lions' den. Now this rebel has broken the substance of these laws, not only in thought (which is bad enough), but also in word and deed, which is intolerable.

"In the case of Pharaoh, his law was based upon a supposition, to prevent mischief, since no crime was yet apparent; but here a crime is apparent. In regard to the second and third instances, you can see that he argues against our religion; and for the treason he has confessed to, he deserves to die."

Then the jury, whose names were Mr. Blind-man, Mr. No-good, Mr. Malice, Mr. Love-lust, Mr. Live-loose, Mr. Heady, Mr.

High-mind, Mr. Enmity, Mr. Liar, Mr. Cruelty, Mr. Hate-light, and Mr. Implacable, went out to deliberate; each one gave his private verdict against Faithful, and afterward they unanimously found him guilty. First, among themselves, Mr. Blind-man, the foreman, said, "I see clearly that this man is a heretic." Then said Mr. No-good, "Rid the earth of the fellow!" "I agree," said Mr. Malice, "for I hate the very sight of him." Then Mr. Love-lust said, "I never could stand him." "Nor I," said Mr. Live-loose, "for he was always condemning me." "Hang him, hang him!" said Mr. Heady. "A sorry scrub," said Mr. High-mind. "My heart rises against him," said Mr. Enmity. "He is a rogue," said Mr. Liar. "Hanging is too good for him," said Mr. Cruelty. "Let us get rid of him," said Mr. Hate-light. Then Mr. Implacable said, "Even if all the world were given to me, I could not accept him; therefore let us immediately bring in a verdict of guilty and a sentence of death." And so they did.

Therefore, Faithful was condemned to the most cruel death that could be invented.

They brought him out then, to punish him according to their law; and first they scourged him, then they buffeted him, then they lanced his flesh with knives; after that they stoned him with stones, then pricked him with their swords; and last of all they burned him to ashes at the stake. And thus came Faithful to his death.

Now I saw that there stood behind the multitude a chariot and a couple of horses, waiting for Faithful, who (as soon as his adversaries had killed him) was taken up into it and immediately carried up through the clouds, with sound of trumpets, the nearest way to the Celestial Gate.

> *Brave Faithful, bravely done in word and deed;*
> *Judge, witnesses, and jury have, instead*
> *Of overcoming thee, but shown their rage;*
> *When they are dead, thou'lt live from age to age.*

But as for Christian, he had some reprieve and was returned to prison. There he remained for a time; but he who overrules all things, having the power of their rage in his own hand, enabled Christian to escape them and to continue on his way. And as he went, he sang:

Well, Faithful, thou hast faithfully professed
Unto thy Lord; with whom thou shalt be blest,
When faithless ones, with all their vain delights,
Are crying out under their hellish plights:
Sing, Faithful, sing, and let thy name survive;
For though they killed thee, thou art yet alive.

Now I saw in my dream that Christian did not go on alone, for Hopeful, who had been won to the Lord by the words and behavior of Christian and Faithful in their sufferings at the fair, joined him and promised that he would be his companion. Thus one died to bear testimony to the truth and another rose out of his ashes to be a companion to Christian on his pilgrimage. Hopeful also told Christian that there were many more men in the fair who would eventually follow them.

Shortly after they had left the fair, they overtook someone who was ahead of them, whose name was By-ends. So they said to him, "What country are you from, sir, and how far are you going?" He told them that he came from the town of Fair-speech and was going to the Celestial City, but he did not tell them his name.

"From Fair-speech?" said Christian. "Is there anything good there?"

BY-ENDS: Yes, I hope so.

CHRISTIAN: Tell me, sir, what may I call you?

BY-ENDS: I am a stranger to you, and you to me. If you are going this way, I shall be glad of your company; if not, I must be content.

CHRISTIAN: I have heard of this town of Fair-speech, and as I remember, they say it's a wealthy place.

BY-ENDS: Yes, I assure you that it is, and I have many rich relatives there.

CHRISTIAN: Who are your relatives there, if I may be so bold?

BY-ENDS: Almost the whole town; and in particular, Lord Turn-about, Lord Time-server, Lord Fair-speech (from whose ancestors that town first took its name), also Mr. Smooth-man, Mr. Facing-both-ways, Mr. Anything; and the parson of our parish, Mr. Two-tongues, was my mother's own brother. To tell you the truth, my great-grandfather was only a boatman, looking one way and rowing another, and I got most of my wealth by the same occupation.

CHRISTIAN: Are you a married man?

BY-ENDS: Yes, and my wife is a very virtuous woman, and is the daughter of a virtuous woman. She was Lady Feigning's daughter; therefore, she came of a very honorable family, and has so much breeding that she knows how to deal with anyone, from prince to peasant. It is true that we differ somewhat in religion from those of the stricter sort, yet only in two small points: first, we never go against the wind and the tide; and second, we are always most zealous when religion walks in silver slippers and when the sun shines and the people applaud what we believe. Then Christian stepped aside with Hopeful and said, "It occurs to me that this is By-ends of Fair-speech; and if it is, we have in our company one of the most deceitful fellows in this land." Then said Hopeful, "Ask him. I should think he wouldn't be ashamed of his name." So Christian went up to him again and said, "Sir, you talk as if you knew more than anybody else, and if I am not mistaken, I believe I know who you are. Isn't your name Mr. By-ends of Fair-speech?"

BY-ENDS: That is not my name, but it is a nickname given me by some who do not like me; and I must be content to bear it as a reproach, as other good men before me have done.

CHRISTIAN: Did you never give men a reason to call you by this name?

BY-ENDS: Never, never! The worst I ever did to give them a reason to call me this was that I was always lucky enough to go with the tide, whatever it was, and thereby gain the advantage; and if things go my way, let me count them a blessing; but the malicious should not therefore heap me with reproach.

CHRISTIAN: I thought you were the man I had heard of; and to tell you what I think, I fear this name belongs to you more than you are willing to admit.

BY-ENDS: Well, if you want to think so, I cannot help it; you will find me good company if you will still let me associate with you.

CHRISTIAN: If you want to go with us, you must go against wind and tide, which, I see, is against your beliefs; you must also own religion when it is in rags, as well as when it is in silver slippers, and stand by it when it is bound in irons, as well as when it is applauded in the streets.

BY-ENDS: You must not impose your beliefs on me, nor lord it over my faith; leave me my freedom, and let me go with you.

CHRISTIAN: Do not take a step further, unless you will do as we do.

BY-ENDS: I shall never desert my old principles, since they are harmless and profitable. If I may not go with you, I must go by myself, until someone overtakes me who will be glad of my company.

Now I saw in my dream that Christian and Hopeful left him and kept their distance in front of him; but one of them, looking back, saw three men following Mr. By-ends, and as they caught up with him, he made a very low bow toward Christian and Hopeful, as though dismissing them. The men's names were Mr. Hold-the-world, Mr. Money-love, and Mr. Save-all, all men that Mr. By-ends had formerly been acquainted with; for when they were young they had been schoolmates and were taught by Mr. Gripe-man, a teacher in Love-gain, which is a town in the county of Coveting in the north. This schoolmaster taught them the art of getting, either by violence, cheating, flattery, lying, or by putting on a guise of religion; and these four gentlemen had learned the art of their master so well that they could have conducted such a school themselves.

Well, when they had greeted each other, Mr. Money-love said to Mr. By-ends, "Who are those two in front of us?" (for Christian and Hopeful were still within view).

BY-ENDS: They are a couple of our distant countrymen who are going on pilgrimage.

MONEY-LOVE: Why didn't they wait so that we could enjoy their company? For all of us, I hope, are going on pilgrimage.

BY-ENDS: We are indeed. But the men in front of us are so rigid, and love their own beliefs so much, and think so little of the opinions of others, that even if a man is ever so godly, if he does not agree with them in all things, they do not want him with them.

SAVE-ALL: That is too bad, but we have read of some who are overly righteous; and such men's rigidness causes them to judge and condemn all but themselves. But tell me, what were the things on which you differed?

BY-ENDS: Why, in their headstrong manner, they believe it is their duty to hurry on their journey in all kinds of weather, and I am for waiting until the wind and tide are with me. They think you should risk all for God, and I believe in taking every advantage to make sure my life and worldly goods are secure. They are for holding to their beliefs, though all other men are against them; but I am for religion as long as the times and my safety will bear it. They are for religion when it is in rags and held in contempt, but I am for it when it walks in golden slippers in the sunshine and with applause.

MR. HOLD-THE-WORLD: Hold fast to that, good Mr. By-ends; for I consider anyone a fool who, having the freedom to keep what he has, is so unwise as to lose it. Let us be as wise as serpents; it is best to make hay when the sun shines; you see how the bee lies still all winter, and stirs only when she can do so with profit and pleasure. God sometimes sends rain and sometimes sunshine; if they are foolish enough to go through the first, then let us be content to take the fair weather. For my part, I like that religion best that represents the security of God's blessings to us; since God has given us the good things of this life, why would he not want us to keep them for his sake? Abraham and Solomon grew rich in religion. And Job says that a good man shall lay up gold like dust. But he must not have been like the men before us, if they are as you have described them.

MR. SAVE-ALL: I think we are all agreed in this matter, and therefore we don't need to discuss it further.

MR. MONEY-LOVE: No, we need no more words about this matter indeed; for he who believes neither Scripture nor reason (and you see we have both on our side) neither knows his own freedom, nor seeks his own safety.

MR. BY-ENDS: My brothers, we are all going on pilgrimage; and to take our minds off such negative things, let me propose this question:

Suppose a man—a minister or a shopkeeper—should have the opportunity to get the good blessings of this life, but only if he, in appearance at least, becomes extraordinarily zealous about some points of religion that he has not concerned himself with before; may he not use this means to attain his end and still be an honest man?

MR. MONEY-LOVE: I see the essential meaning of your question; and with these gentlemen's permission, I will endeavor to formulate an answer. First, to speak to your question as it concerns a minister himself: Suppose a minister, a worthy man, possesses a very small benefice and desires a greater one by far; he now has an opportunity of getting it by being more studious, by preaching more frequently and zealously, and, because the nature of the people requires it, by altering some of his principles; for my part, I see no reason why a man may not do this (provided he has a call), and a great deal more besides, and still be an honest man. For

1. His desire for a greater benefice is lawful (this cannot be contradicted), since it is set before him by Providence; so then he may get it, if he can, without raising questions of conscience.

2. Besides, his desire for that benefice will make him more studious, a more zealous preacher, and thus a better man; yes, it makes him improve himself, which is according to the mind of God.

3. Now as for his complying with the desires of his people, to serve them, by altering some of his principles, this shows that he has a self-denying temperament, a sweet and winning manner, and is all the more fit to function as a minister.

4. I conclude, then, that a minister who changes a small benefice for a great should not be judged as covetous for doing so; but rather, since he has thereby improved himself and his work, he should be counted as one who pursues his call and the opportunity given him to do good.

And now to the second part of the question, which concerns the shopkeeper you mentioned. Suppose such a person has had only a small business, but by becoming religious he may increase the size of his shop, perhaps get a rich wife, or bring more and far better customers to his shop; for my part, I see no reason why this may not be lawfully done. For

1. To become religious is a virtue, no matter by what means a man becomes so.

2. Nor is it unlawful to get a rich wife or more customers to his shop.

3. Besides, the man who gets these by becoming religious, gets that which is good from those who are good by becoming good himself; so here is a good wife, and good customers, and good gain, and all these by becoming religious, which is good; therefore to become religious to get all these is a good and profitable plan.

This answer given by Mr. Money-love to Mr. By-ends's question was applauded by all of them; therefore they concluded that it was wholesome and advantageous. And because they thought no man was able to contradict it, and because Christian and Hopeful were still within the sound of their voices, they agreed to throw the question at them as soon as they overtook them because Christian and Hopeful had opposed Mr. By-ends before. So they called after them, and the two men stopped and waited. But the four decided, as they walked, that old Mr. Hold-the-world, not Mr. By-ends, should propose the question, because they figured Christian's and Hopeful's answer to him would not be subject to the strong feelings that had been aroused between them and Mr. By-ends at their earlier parting.

So they came up to each other, and after a short greeting, Mr. Hold-the-world raised the question to Christian and Hopeful and asked them to answer it if they could.

CHRISTIAN: Even a babe in religion may answer ten thousand such questions. For if it is unlawful to follow Christ for loaves, as it is, how much more abominable is it to make him and religion a stalking-horse to promote themselves or their business. Only heathens, hypocrites, devils, and witches think this way.

1. For when the heathens Hamor and Shechem wanted the daughter and cattle of Jacob and saw that there was no way to get them except by becoming circumcised, they said to

their companions: If each of our males is circumcised as they are circumcised, will not their cattle, and their substance, and every beast of theirs be ours? They wanted Jacob's daughter and cattle, and Jacob's religion was the stalking-horse they made use of to get them. Read the whole story.

2. The hypocritical Pharisees were also of this religion; long prayers were their pretense, but to get the widows' houses was their intent; and greater damnation from God was their judgment.

3. Judas the devil was also of this religion; he was religious for the bag of money so that he might possess what was therein; but he was lost, cast away, and the very son of perdition.

4. Simon the witch was of this religion too; for he wanted the Holy Ghost in order to get money; and he was sentenced accordingly from Peter's mouth.

5. The man who takes up religion for the world will throw away religion for the world; for as surely as Judas resigned the world in becoming religious, so surely did he also sell religion and his Master for the same. Therefore, to answer the question affirmatively, as I see you have done, and to accept such an answer as authentic, is heathenish, hypocritical, and devilish; and you will be rewarded accordingly.

Then they stood staring at one another, but had no way to answer Christian. Hopeful also agreed with the truth of Christian's answer; so there was a great silence among them. Mr. By-ends and his company hesitated and lagged behind so that Christian and Hopeful might go ahead of them. Then said Christian to his friend, "If these men cannot stand before the judgment of men, what will they do with the judgment of God? And if they are silent when dealt with by vessels of clay, what will they do when they are rebuked by the flames of a devouring fire?"

Then Christian and Hopeful went ahead of them again and traveled until they came to a pleasant plain called Ease, where they walked with great contentment; but the plain was very narrow, so they crossed it quickly. Now at the far side of that plain was a little hill called Lucre, and in that hill was a silver mine, which some who had previously passed that way had turned aside to see because of its rarity; but when they got too close to the edge of the pit, the ground gave way under them and they were killed; some also had been maimed there and were never the same to their dying day.

Then I saw in my dream that a little off the road, beside the silver mine, stood Demas, calling politely for travelers to come and see; he said to Christian and Hopeful, "Hello there! Come over here and I will show you something."

CHRISTIAN: What could be worthwhile enough to make us leave the way?

DEMAS: There is a silver mine here, and some are digging in it for treasure. If you will come, with very little effort you may richly provide for yourselves.

HOPEFUL: Let us go see.

CHRISTIAN: Not I. I have heard of this place before, and how many have been killed here; and besides that, treasure is a trap to those who seek it, for it hinders them in their pilgrimage.

Then Christian called to Demas, "Isn't this place dangerous? Hasn't it hindered many in their pilgrimage?"

DEMAS: Not very dangerous, except to those who are careless (but he blushed as he said this).

CHRISTIAN: Let us not move a step toward it, but keep on our way.

HOPEFUL: I will guarantee you that when By-ends comes up, if he receives this same invitation, he will turn in there to look at it.

CHRISTIAN: No doubt he will, for his principles lead him that way, and a hundred to one he dies there.

Then Demas called again, saying, "But will you not come over and see?"

Then Christian rebuked him, saying, "Demas, you are an enemy to the right ways of the Lord of this way, and have been condemned already for your own waywardness by one of His Majesty's judges. Why do you try to bring us into the same condemnation? Besides, if we turn aside at all, our Lord the King will certainly hear of it and will put us to shame, and we desire to stand with boldness before him."

Demas cried that he also was one of their brothers, and that if they would wait a little while, he would walk with them.

CHRISTIAN: What is your name? Is it not the name I have called you?

DEMAS: Yes, my name is Demas; I am the son of Abraham.

CHRISTIAN: I know you. Gehazi was your great-grandfather, and Judas your father; and you have walked in their steps. It is a devilish prank that you use; your father was hanged as a traitor, and you deserve no better reward. You may be assured that when we come to the King, we will tell him about your behavior.

Thus they went their way.

By this time By-ends and his companions were again within sight, and I saw that they went over to Demas the first time he called to them. Now whether they fell into the pit by looking over the brink, or whether they went down to dig, or whether they were smothered in the bottom by the poisonous gases, I am not certain; but I did observe that they were never seen again in the way. Then Christian sang:

By-ends and silver Demas both agree;
One calls, the other runs, that he may be
A sharer in his lucre; so these do
Take up in this world, and no further go.

Now I saw that just on the other side of this plain the pilgrims came to a place where there stood an old monument, right beside the highway, at the sight of which they were both concerned because of its strange form, for it looked to them like a woman transformed into the shape of a pillar; they stood looking at it for a long time but could not tell what it was. At last Hopeful spied something written on the head of it in an unusual script; but he, being no scholar, called to Christian (for he was well-educated) to see if he could figure out the meaning; so he came and finally found that the words said, "Remember Lot's wife." So he read it to Hopeful, after which they concluded that this was the pillar of salt into which Lot's wife was turned when she was fleeing from Sodom and looked back with a covetous heart. This unexpected and amazing sight gave rise to this conversation between them.

CHRISTIAN: Ah, my brother! This sight came at an opportune time, right after the invitation Demas gave us to come over to view the Hill Lucre; and had we gone over as he desired, and as you were inclined to do, my brother, we would have, for all I know, been like this woman ourselves, a spectacle for those who come after us.

HOPEFUL: I am sorry I was so foolish, and it makes me wonder why I am not like Lot's wife now; for what was the difference between her sin and mine? She only looked back; and I had a desire to go look. Let grace be revered, and let me be ashamed that such desires should ever have been in my heart.

CHRISTIAN: Let us take note of what we see here for our help in the future. This woman escaped one judgment, for she did not die in the destruction of Sodom; yet she was destroyed by another, as we see, for she was turned into a pillar of salt.

HOPEFUL: True. And she may be both a warning and example to us: a warning that we should shun her sin, and an example of what judgment will be ours if we do not heed that warning, just as Korah, Dathan, and Abiram, with the two hundred and fifty men that perished in their sin, became a sign or example to others to beware. But above all, I marvel at one thing, and that is how Demas and his companions can stand so confidently looking for that treasure for which this woman, who only looked behind her but did not step one foot out of the way, was turned into a pillar of salt; especially since the judgment which overtook her made her an example within sight of where they are; for they cannot help but see her if they only lift up their eyes.

CHRISTIAN: It is something to be wondered at, and it seems to indicate that their hearts are desperately sinful; and I cannot help but compare them to those who pick pockets in the presence of the judge, or that cut purses right under the gallows. It is said that the men of Sodom "were sinners exceedingly" because they were sinners "before the Lord"; that is, in his eyesight and notwithstanding the kindnesses he had showed them; for the land of Sodom was at that time like the Garden of Eden. This provoked him all the more to jealousy, and made their plague as hot as the fire of the Lord in heaven could make it. And it can logically be concluded then that those who sin within sight of and in spite of such examples set continually before them, to caution them to the contrary, shall be judged the most severely.

HOPEFUL: Doubtless you have spoken the truth; but what a mercy it is that neither you nor I, especially I, have been made an example like this. It is an occasion for us to thank God, to fear him, and always to remember Lot's wife.

I saw then that they went on their way to a pleasant river, which David the king called "the river of God," but which John called the "river of the water of life." Now their path lay just along the bank of the river, and here Christian and his companion walked with great delight; they also drank the water of the river, which was pleasant and enlivening to their weary spirits. On the banks of this river, on either side, were green trees that bore all kinds of fruit, and the leaves of the trees had healing qualities. They were delighted with the fruit of these trees, and they ate the leaves to prevent illness from overindulgence and other diseases to which travelers are susceptible. On either side of the river was a meadow filled with beautiful lilies, and it was green all the year long. In this meadow they lay down and slept, for here they could rest safely. When they awoke, they again gathered the fruit of the trees, and drank the water of the river, and then lay down again to sleep. This they did for several days and nights. Then they sang:

> *Behold ye how these crystal streams do glide*
> *(To comfort pilgrims) by the highway side;*
> *The meadows green, besides their fragrant smell,*
> *Yield dainties for them: and he that can tell*
> *What pleasant fruit, yea, leaves, these trees do yield,*
> *Will soon sell all, that he may buy this field.*

So when they felt ready to go on (for they were not, as yet, at their journey's end), they ate and drank and departed.

Now I beheld in my dream that they had not journeyed far when the river and the path separated for a time; they were rather sad about this, but they dared not leave the path. Then the path away from the river became rough, and their feet became tender from walking; "so the souls of the pilgrims were much discouraged because of the way." Therefore, they wished for a better pathway. Now a little ahead of them there was on the left-hand side of the road a meadow, and a set of steps by which to cross over the fence into it; and that meadow is called By-path Meadow. Then Christian said to his friend, "If this meadow lies alongside our pathway, let's go over into it." Then he climbed the steps to see, and, behold, there was a path running along the other side of the fence. "It's just what I was wishing for," said Christian. "Here it is much easier going. Come, good Hopeful, let's go over."

HOPEFUL: But what if this path should lead us out of the way?

CHRISTIAN: That's not likely. Look, doesn't it go along parallel to the pathway?

So Hopeful, being persuaded by his friend, followed him over the fence, and they found this path very easy for their feet. Then, looking ahead, they spied a man walking as they did (and his name was Vain-confidence); so they called out to him and asked him where this path led. He said, "To the Celestial Gate." "Look," said Christian, "didn't I tell you so? See, we are right." So they followed, and Vain-confidence went before them. But behold, night came on and it grew very dark and they lost sight of the man ahead of them.

> *The pilgrims now, to gratify the flesh,*
> *Will seek its ease; but oh! how they afresh*
> *Do thereby plunge themselves new grief into!*
> *Who seek to please the flesh, themselves undo.*

Therefore, the one who was ahead of them, not being able to see the pathway, fell into a deep pit, which was put there purposely by the prince of those grounds to catch vain-glorious fools, and he was dashed in pieces by the fall.

Now Christian and Hopeful heard him fall. So they called out, asking what had happened, but there was no answer, only a groaning sound. Then said Hopeful, "Where are we now?" But his companion was silent, afraid that he had led him out of the way; and now it began to rain and thunder and lightning in a dreadful manner, and the pathway began to flood.

Then Hopeful groaned in himself, saying, "Oh, I wish I had kept on my way!"

CHRISTIAN: Who could have thought that this path would lead us out of the way?

HOPEFUL: I was afraid of it from the very first, and that is why I was cautious. I would have spoken plainer, except that you are older than I.

CHRISTIAN: Good brother, don't be offended. I am sorry I have brought you out of the way and put you in such imminent danger. Please forgive me, my brother; I did not do it with any evil intentions.

HOPEFUL: Be comforted, my brother, for I forgive you; and I also believe that this shall be for our good.

CHRISTIAN: I am glad I have a merciful brother with me. But we must not stand here like this. Let's try to go back again.

HOPEFUL: Let me walk in front, good brother.

CHRISTIAN: No, if you please, let me go first, so that if there is any danger I will be the first to encounter it, because it is my fault that we have both left the way.

HOPEFUL: No, you shall not go first. You are upset, and this may cause you to lead us astray again.

Then for their encouragement they heard the voice of one saying, "Let thine heart be towards the highway, even the way that thou wentest, turn again." But by this time the waters had risen greatly, making the pathway back very dangerous. (Then I thought: it is easier to get out of the way when we are in it, than to get in when we are out.) Yet they tried to go back; but it was so dark, and the flood was so high, that in going back they were almost drowned nine or ten times.

Neither could they, with all the skill they had, get back that night to the place where they had crossed the fence. At last, finding a little shelter, they sat down to rest until morning; but, being weary, they fell asleep.

Now there was, not far from the place where they lay, a castle called Doubting Castle, owned by Giant Despair, and it was on his land that they were sleeping. Therefore, when he got up early in the morning and walked up and down in his fields, he caught Christian and Hopeful asleep on his property. Then with a grim and surly voice he told them to wake up and asked them where they had come from and what they were doing on his land. They told him they were pilgrims and that they had lost their way. Then said the giant, "You have trespassed on me by trampling in and lying on my grounds, and therefore you must go along with me." So they were forced to go, because he was stronger than they. They also had little to say because they knew they were at fault. The giant prodded them on before him and put them into a dark dungeon inside his castle, a nasty and stinking place to the spirits of these two men. Here they lay from Wednesday morning till Saturday night, without one bite of bread, or drop of water, or light, or anyone to ask how they were; thus they were in this evil situation, far from friends and acquaintances. Now in this place Christian had double sorrow, because it was through his ill-advised haste that they had gotten into this trouble.

Now Giant Despair had a wife, and her name was Diffidence. So when he went to bed, he told his wife what he had done; that is, that he had taken a couple of prisoners and cast them into his dungeon for trespassing on his grounds. Then he asked her what he should do with them. So she asked him who they were, where they came from, and where they were going; and he told her. Then she advised him to beat them without mercy in the morning.

So when he arose, he got a heavy club made from the wood of a crab-tree, and he went down into the dungeon to the prisoners. First he scolded them as if they were dogs, although they never spoke a word of complaint to him. Then he beat them so badly that they were unable to move. After this, he left them in their misery. So all that day they did nothing but sigh and moan bitterly. The next night the wife, in talking with her husband about them further and learning they were still alive, advised him to counsel them to kill themselves. So in the morning he went to them in a surly manner as he had before, and seeing they were very sore from the beating he had given them the day before, he told them that since they were never likely to get out of that place, their only escape was to do away with themselves, either with knife, rope, or poison. "For why," said he, "should you choose life, since it is filled with so much bitterness?" But they asked him to let them go. With that he gave them an ugly look and rushed at them and no doubt would have killed them himself, except that he fell into one of his fits (for he sometimes in sunshiny weather fell into fits), and lost the use of his hand for a time; therefore he withdrew and left them as before to consider what to do. Then the prisoners discussed whether or not they should take his advice.

CHRISTIAN: Brother, what shall we do? The life we now live is miserable. For my part, I don't know whether it is better to live this way or to die without delay. "My soul chooseth strangling rather than life," and the grave looks better to me than this dungeon. Shall we take the giant's advice?

HOPEFUL: Indeed our present condition is dreadful, and death would be far more welcome to me than to live like this forever. But let us remember that the Lord of the country to which we are going has said, "You shall not kill another person"; much more then are we forbidden to take his advice to kill ourselves. Besides, he who kills another only commits murder upon his body; but one who kills himself kills both body and soul. And moreover, my brother, you talk of ease in the grave; but have you forgotten the Hell where murderers go? For "no murderer has eternal life."

And let us consider again that all the law is not in the hand of Giant Despair. Others, as far as I can understand, have also been captured by him, yet have escaped. Who knows but that God who made the world may cause the death of Giant Despair? Or that at some time or other he may forget to lock us in? Or he may soon have another of his fits and lose the use of his limbs? And if ever that should happen again, I am resolved to take heart and try my utmost to get away from him. I was a fool not to try to do it before; but, my brother, let's be patient and endure for a while longer. In time we may escape. But let us not be our own murderers.

With these words, Hopeful calmed his brother, and they endured the dark together that day, in their sad condition.

Well toward evening the giant went down into the dungeon again to see if his prisoners had taken his advice. But when he got there, he found them alive; and barely alive was all, for what with lack of bread and water and by reason of the wounds they had received when he beat them, they could do little but breathe. But he did find them alive, at which he fell into a terrible rage and told them that since they had disobeyed his counsel, they were going to wish they had never been born.

At this they trembled greatly, and Christian fainted. But after he had revived a little, they once more began to discuss whether or not they had better take the giant's advice. Now Christian again seemed to be in favor of doing this, but Hopeful replied, "My brother, don't you remember how brave you have been heretofore? Apollyon could not crush you, nor could all that you heard and saw and felt in the Valley of the Shadow of Death. Think about the hardship, terror, and bewilderment you have already gone through. You see that I am in the dungeon with you, a far weaker man by nature than you are; also, this giant has wounded me as well as you and has also refused me bread and water; and with you I mourn without the light. But let us exercise a little more patience; remember how brave you were at Vanity Fair, and were neither afraid of the chain, nor the cage, nor even bloody death. Therefore let us at least avoid the shame that is unbecoming to a Christian and bear up with patience as well as we can."

Now night had come again, and the giant and his wife were in bed, and she asked him about the prisoners, whether they had taken his counsel. To which he replied, "They are rugged scoundrels. They would rather bear the hardship than kill themselves." Then said she, "Take them into the castle yard tomorrow and show them the bones and skulls of those you have already killed, and make them believe that before the week is out you will also tear them in pieces, as you have done to those before them."

So in the morning the giant went to them again and took them into the castle yard and showed them, as his wife had told him. "These once were pilgrims as you are," said he, "and they trespassed on my property as you have done; and when I thought fit, I tore them in pieces; and so will I do to you within ten days. Go! Get down to your dungeon again!" And with that he beat them all the way there. Therefore, all day Saturday they lay in a deplorable state, as they had before.

Now when night fell and Mrs. Diffidence and her husband Despair had gone to bed, they once more discussed their prisoners; and the old giant marveled that he could neither by his blows nor his counsel bring them to an end. And with that his wife replied, "I fear that they live in hope that someone will come to relieve them, or that they have lockpicks with them, by the means of which they hope to escape." "Do you think so, my dear?" said the giant. "In that case, I will search them in the morning."

Well, on Saturday about midnight they began to pray, and continued in prayer till almost the break of day.

Now a little before daylight, good Christian broke out in this passionate speech: "What a fool I am to lie in a stinking dungeon when I can freely walk away! I have a key in my bosom called Promise, that will, I am persuaded, open any lock in Doubting Castle." Then said Hopeful, "That is good news, good brother; pull it out of your bosom and try."

Then Christian pulled out the key of Promise and began to try the dungeon door; and as he turned it, the bolt slid back and the door flew open with ease, and Christian and Hopeful both came out. Then he went to the outer door that led into the castle yard, and with his key opened that door also. After that he went to the iron gate, for that must be opened too; that lock was very hard to turn, yet the key did open it. Then they threw open the gate to make their escape quickly, but that gate made such a creaking noise as it opened that it roused Giant Despair. He rose hastily to pursue his prisoners, but felt his legs fail, for one of his fits took him again, so that he could not go after them. So Christian and Hopeful went on and came to the King's highway, and thus were safe because they were out of Despair's jurisdiction.

Now when they had gone back over the fence at the stairs where they had originally crossed, they began to consider how they might prevent others from crossing there and falling into the hands of Giant Despair. So they decided to erect a pillar there and engrave this sentence upon the side: "Over these steps is the way to Doubting Castle, which is kept by Giant Despair, who despises the King of the Celestial Country and seeks to destroy his holy pilgrims." Because of this, many who followed after read what was written and escaped the danger. This done, they sang:

Out of the way we went, and then we found
What 'twas to tread upon forbidden ground;
And let them that come after have a care,
Lest heedlessness makes them, as we, to fare.
Lest they for trespassing his prisoners are,
Whose castle's Doubting and whose name's Despair.

Christian and Hopeful traveled until they came to the Delectable Mountains, which belonged to the Lord of that hill of which we have spoken before; they went up to the mountains to look at the gardens and orchards, the vineyards, and the fountains of water, where they drank and washed themselves and ate freely from the vineyards. Now on the tops of these mountains, near the pathway, were Shepherds tending their flocks. The two pilgrims approached them and, leaning upon their staffs (as weary pilgrims usually do when they stand to talk with anyone by the way), asked, "Who do these Delectable Mountains belong to? And who owns the sheep that graze upon them?"

Mountains delectable they now ascend,
Where Shepherds be, which to them do commend
Alluring things, and things that cautious are,
Pilgrims are steady kept by faith and fear.

SHEPHERD: These mountains are Immanuel's Land, and they are within sight of his city; the sheep are also his, and he laid down his life for them.

CHRISTIAN: Is this the way to the Celestial City?

SHEPHERD: You are just on the path.

CHRISTIAN: How far is it?

SHEPHERD: Too far for any but those who really want to get there.

CHRISTIAN: Is the way safe or dangerous?

SHEPHERD: Safe for those for whom it is to be safe; "but transgressors shall fall therein."

CHRISTIAN: Is there any relief in this place for pilgrims who are weary and faint?

SHEPHERD: The Lord of these mountains has ordered us to entertain strangers; therefore the good things of this place are available to you.

I saw also in my dream that when the Shepherds perceived that they were wayfarers, they questioned them (which they answered as they had in other places) with such questions as, "Where did you come from?" and, "How did you get into the way?" and, "By what means have you persevered? For few of those who begin the journey to this place ever show their face on these mountains." But when the Shepherds heard their answers, they were pleased and looked very lovingly upon them and said, "Welcome to the Delectable Mountains."

The Shepherds, whose names were Knowledge, Experience, Watchful, and Sincere, took them by the hand and led them to their tents and made them partake of that which had been prepared for them. They said, moreover, "We would like you to stay here a while so you can get acquainted with us; and more than that, so you can comfort yourselves with the good of these Delectable Mountains." Christian and Hopeful told them that they were content to stay; so they went to rest that night, because it was very late.

In the morning the Shepherds called to Christian and Hopeful to walk with them upon the mountains; so they walked with them for a while, admiring the pleasant view on every side. Then the Shepherds said to one another, "Shall we show these pilgrims some wonders?" When they had agreed to do this, they took them first to the top of a hill called Error, which was very steep on the far side, and told them to look down to the bottom. So Christian and Hopeful looked down and saw at the bottom several men who had been smashed to pieces by a fall from the top. Then said Christian, "What does this mean?" And the Shepherds answered, "Have you not heard of those who were caused to err by listening to Hymenaeus and Philetus concerning the faith of the resurrection of the body?" They answered, "Yes." Then said the Shepherds, "They are the ones you see smashed to pieces at the bottom of this mountain; and they lie there to this day unburied, as you see, as an example to others to be careful lest they climb too high or come too near the brink of this mountain."

Then I saw that they led them to the top of another mountain, named Caution, and told them to look off into the distance. When they did, they saw several men walking up and down among the tombs that were there; and they realized that the men were blind, because they stumbled sometimes upon the tombs and could not get out from among them. Then said Christian, "What does this mean?"

The Shepherds answered, "Did you not see a little below these mountains some steps that led into a meadow, on the left side of this way?" They answered, "Yes." Then said the Shepherds, "From those steps goes a path that leads directly to Doubting Castle, which is kept by Giant Despair, and these men (and they pointed to the men among the tombs) were once on pilgrimage, as you are now, until they came to those steps; and because the right way was rough in that place, they chose to leave it and go into that meadow, and there they were taken by Giant Despair and cast into Doubting Castle; where, after they had been kept in the dungeon a while, he at last put out their eyes and led them among these tombs, where he has left them to wander to this very day, so that the saying of the wise man might be fulfilled, 'He that wandereth out of the way of understanding shall remain in the congregation of the dead.'" Then Christian and Hopeful looked at one another with tears pouring down their cheeks, but said nothing to the Shepherds.

Then I saw in my dream that the Shepherds took them to another place, in the bottom of a valley, where there was a door in the side of a hill; and they opened the door and told them to look in. They looked in and saw that it was very dark and smoky; they also thought that they heard a rumbling noise like fire, and a cry of torment, and the scent of brimstone. Then said Christian, "What does this mean?" The Shepherds told them, "This is another road to hell, a way that hypocrites take; like those who sell their birthright, with Esau; like those who sell their master, with Judas; like those who blaspheme the gospel, with Alexander; and like those who lie and dissemble, with Ananias and his wife."

Then Hopeful said to the Shepherds, "Every one of these appeared to be on pilgrimage, as we are now, did they not?"

SHEPHERD: Yes, and held to it for a long time.

HOPEFUL: How far did they go on pilgrimage in their day, since they were so miserably cast away?

SHEPHERD: Some went further than these mountains, and some did not get this far.

Then the pilgrims said to each other, "We had better cry to the Strong for strength."

SHEPHERDS: Yes, and you will need to use it when you have it too.

By this time the pilgrims desired to go forward, and the Shepherds desired that they should; so they walked together toward the end of the mountains. Then the Shepherds said to one another, "Let us show the pilgrims the gates of the Celestial City, if they are able to look through our telescope." The pilgrims gratefully accepted the suggestion; so the Shepherds led them to the top of a high hill called Clear and gave them their glass to look through.

Then they attempted to look, but the memory of the last thing the Shepherds had shown them made their hands shake; because of this impediment they could not look steadily through the glass; yet they thought they saw something like the gate and some of the glory of the place. Then they went away singing this song:

Thus by the Shepherds secrets are revealed,
Which from all other men are kept concealed.
Come to the Shepherds then, if you would see
Things deep, things hid, and that mysterious be.

When they were about to depart, one of the Shepherds gave them a map of the way. Another warned them to beware of the Flatterer. The third told them not to sleep upon the Enchanted Ground. And the fourth bid them God-speed. So I awoke from my dream.

Then I slept and dreamed again, and I saw the same two pilgrims going down the mountains along the highway toward the city. Now a little below these mountains, on the left hand, lay the country of Conceit; and a little crooked lane led from this country into the way in which the pilgrims walked. Here they encountered a very energetic lad who had come out of that country, and his name was Ignorance. So Christian asked him where he came from and where he was going.

IGNORANCE: Sir, I was born in the country that lies off there a little on the left, and I am going to the Celestial City.

CHRISTIAN: But how do you plan to get in at the gate, for you may find some difficulty there?

IGNORANCE: I will get in as other good people do.

CHRISTIAN: But what do you have to show at the gate that may cause the gate to be opened to you?

IGNORANCE: I know my Lord's will, and I have lived a good life. I pay every man what I owe him; I pray, fast, tithe, and give to the poor; and I have left my country to go there.

CHRISTIAN: But you did not come in at the wicket-gate at the beginning of this way; you came in through that crooked lane, and therefore I fear that regardless of what you may think of yourself, when the day of judgment comes you will be charged with being a thief and a robber, instead of being admitted to the city.

IGNORANCE: Gentlemen, you are complete strangers to me; I do not know you. So you follow the religion of your country, and I will follow the religion of mine. I hope all will be well. And as for the gate that you speak of, all the world knows that that is a long ways from our country. I cannot think of anyone in our part of the world who even knows the way to it, nor does it matter whether they do or not since we have, as you see, a fine pleasant green lane that comes down from our country into the way.

When Christian saw that the man was "wise in his own conceit," he whispered to Hopeful, "There is more hope for a fool than for him." And, he added, "When he that is a fool walketh by the way, his wisdom faileth him, and he saith to every one that he is a fool." Shall we talk further with him or go past him and let him think about what we have told him? Then we can wait for him later and see if we can gradually do him any good." Then Hopeful said:

> Let Ignorance a little while now muse
> On what is said, and let him not refuse
> Good counsel to embrace, lest he remain
> Still ignorant of what's the chiefest gain.
> God saith, those that no understanding have
> Although he made them, them he will not save.

HOPEFUL: It is not good to tell him everything at once; let us pass him by and speak with him later, when he is able to bear it.

So they both went on, and Ignorance followed behind. Now when they were a little ways past him, they entered a very dark lane, where they met a man whom seven devils had bound with seven strong cords and were carrying back to the door they had seen on the side of the hill. Now good Christian began to tremble, and so did Hopeful; yet as the devils led the man away, Christian looked to see if he knew him, and he thought it might be Turn-away, who lived in the town of Apostasy. But he did not see his face clearly, for the man hung his head like a thief who had been caught. But once they were past, Hopeful looked back at the man and saw a paper on his back with this inscription, "Wanton professor and damnable apostate."

Then Christian said to his companion, "Now I recall something I was told that happened to a good man around here. His name was Little-faith, but he was a good man, and he lived in the town of Sincere. What happened was this: At the entrance to this passage, a lane comes down from Broad-way Gate called Dead Man's Lane— so called because of the murders that are commonly committed there—and this Little-faith, who was going on pilgrimage as we are, happened to sit down there and fall asleep. Just then three rogues, three brothers named Faint-heart, Mistrust, and Guilt, came down the lane from Broad-way Gate; and spying Little-faith, they came galloping up rapidly. Now the good man had just awakened from his sleep and was preparing to resume his journey when they came up to him and with threatening language ordered him to stand. At this Little-faith turned as white as a sheet and had neither the strength to fight nor to flee. Then said Faint-heart, 'Give us your purse.' But he did not do it, for he did not want to lose his money. So Mistrust ran up to the man and, thrusting his hand into his pocket, pulled out a bag of silver. 'Thieves! Thieves!' cried Little-faith. With that, Guilt struck him on the head with a large club and knocked him flat on the ground, where he lay bleeding like he would bleed to death. All this while the thieves stood by. But at last, hearing someone coming down the road, and fearing that it might be Great-grace from the city of Good-confidence, they ran away, leaving this good man to shift for himself. After a while Little-faith gained consciousness and managed to get to his feet and stumble along on his way."

HOPEFUL: But did they rob him of all that he had?

CHRISTIAN: No. They did not search him thoroughly enough to discover the place where he kept his jewels, so those he still had. But as I was told, the good man was troubled by his loss, for the thieves got most of his spending money. He had a little loose change left, but scarcely enough to take him to his journey's end; no, if I was not misinformed, he was forced to beg as he went, for he could not sell his jewels. But though he begged and did what he could, he went hungry for most of the rest of the way.

HOPEFUL: Isn't it a wonder, though, that they did not get his certificate which was to gain him admittance at the Celestial Gate?

CHRISTIAN: It is a wonder, but they missed it, though not through any cunning of his; for he was so dismayed when they attacked him that he had neither the power nor the skill to hide anything; so it was more by divine Providence than by his own effort that they missed that good thing.

HOPEFUL: But it must have been comforting to him that they did not get his jewels.

CHRISTIAN: It might have been a great comfort to him, had he used it as he should; but those who told me the story said that he made little use of it all the rest of the way because of the dismay he felt over losing his money. Indeed he forgot it for most of the rest of his journey; and besides, when it did come to his mind and he began to be comforted by the thought, then fresh memories of his loss would come upon him again and overwhelm him.

HOPEFUL: Alas, poor man! This must have been a great grief to him.

CHRISTIAN: Grief! yes, grief indeed! Would not any of us have been grieved by such treatment: to be robbed and wounded, and that in a strange place, as he was? It is a wonder he did not die with grief, poor man! I was told that he complained bitterly almost all the rest of the way, telling all he met about how he was robbed and beaten, describing where it had happened, who had done it, what he had lost, and how he had barely escaped with his life.

HOPEFUL: It's a wonder he didn't have to sell or pawn some of his jewels to support himself on the rest of his journey.

CHRISTIAN: You talk like one who was just hatched! What could he pawn them for, or to whom could he sell them? His jewels were of no value in that country where he was robbed, nor did he want that kind of relief. Besides, had his jewels been missing at the gate of the Celestial City, he would have been excluded from an inheritance there, and that he knew very well. For him that would have been worse than the appearance and villainy of ten thousand thieves.

HOPEFUL: Why are you so sharp with me, my brother? Esau sold his birthright for a mess of pottage, and that birthright was his greatest jewel; and if he did, why might not Little-faith do so too?

CHRISTIAN: Indeed, Esau did sell his birthright, and so have many others, and by doing so they exclude themselves from the chief blessing, as that vile coward did; but you must see the difference between Esau and Little-faith, and between their conditions. Esau's birthright was typical, but Little-faith's jewels were not; Esau's god was his belly, but Little-faith's was not; Esau was ruled by his fleshly appetite, but not so Little-faith. Besides, Esau could see no further than the fulfilling of his own lusts; "For I am at the point to die (said he), and what good will this birthright do me?" But Little-faith, though he had only a little faith, was kept from such extravagances by that faith, and made to see and value his jewels so that he would not sell them, as Esau did his birthright. You do not read anywhere that Esau had faith—no, not even a little; therefore it is no wonder that he sold his birthright and his very soul to the Devil, for that is what happens when the flesh rules (as it will in men without faith to resist); for they are like the ass who cannot be restrained during her time of heat. When their minds are focused upon their lusts, they will have them, whatever the cost. But Little-faith was of another temperament; his mind was set on things divine and his existence depended upon things that were spiritual and from above. Therefore what would he gain in selling his jewels (had there been anyone who would have bought them) and filling his mind with empty things? Will a man give a penny to fill his belly with hay; or can you persuade the turtledove to live upon carrion like the crow? Though faithless ones can pawn or mortgage or sell what they have, including their very souls, for carnal lusts, those who have faith, even though it be only a little, cannot do so. Here therefore, my brother, is your mistake.

HOPEFUL: I acknowledge it. But your severe reproach almost made me angry.

CHRISTIAN: Why, I only compared you to some of the young birds who dash about with the shell upon their heads. But ignore that, and consider the matter under discussion, and all shall be well between us.

HOPEFUL: But Christian, I am convinced that these three fellows were just a bunch of cowards; otherwise, do you think they would have run away, as they did, at the sound of someone coming down the road? Why wasn't Little-faith braver? I would think he could have handled at least one skirmish with them, and only yielded if there had been no other choice.

CHRISTIAN: Many have said they are cowards, but few have found it so in the time of trial. As for a great heart, Little-faith had none; and from what you have said, my brother, if it had been you, you would have yielded after just one encounter. And since this is the height of your bravery when they are at a distance from us, should they attack you as they did him, you might have second thoughts.

But remember, they are only hired thieves who serve the king of the bottomless pit, who, if necessary, will come to their rescue himself, and his voice is like the roaring of a lion. I myself have been trapped as Little-faith was, and I found it a terrible thing. Those three villains attacked me, and when I began to resist like a Christian, they gave only one call for help, and in came their master. My life wouldn't have been worth a cent, as the saying goes, except that, as God would have it, I was clothed with armor of proof. And yet even though I was so equipped, I found it hard work to acquit myself like a man. No man can tell what awaits us in that combat unless he has been in the battle himself.

HOPEFUL: But they ran away, you see, when they only imagined that Great-grace was coming their way.

CHRISTIAN: True. Both they and their master have often fled when Great-grace has appeared; and no wonder, for he is the King's champion. But I believe you will see some difference between Little-faith and the King's champion. All the King's subjects are not his champions; nor can they, when tried, accomplish such feats of war as he. Is it right to think that a little child should handle Goliath as David did? Or that a wren should have the strength of an ox? Some are strong; some are weak. Some have great faith; some have little. This man was one of the weak, and therefore he was temporarily overcome.

HOPEFUL: I wish it had been Great-grace for their sakes.

CHRISTIAN: If it had been, he might have had his hands full; for I must tell you that though Great-grace is excellent with his weapons and can handle such fellows well enough as long as he keeps them at sword's point, yet if Faint-heart, Mistrust, or the other get within him, they will eventually knock him down. And when a man is down, what can he do?

Whoever looks carefully at Great-grace's face will see scars and cuts there that are evidence of what I say. Yes, once I heard that he said when he was in combat, "We despaired even of life." These scoundrels made David groan, mourn, and roar. Yes, and Heman and Hezekiah too, though champions in their day, were forced to fight when assaulted by these fellows—and were beaten up by them. At one point Peter went up against them, but of all the apostles, they handled him so skillfully that at last they made him afraid of a weak girl.

Besides, their king is at their beck and call. He is never out of earshot; and if at any time they are getting the worst of it, he, if possible, comes in to help them; and of him it is said, "The sword of him that layeth at him cannot hold: the spear, the dart, nor the [breastplate]. He esteemeth iron as straw, and brass as rotten wood. The arrow cannot make him flee: slingstones are turned with him into stubble. Darts are counted as stubble: he laugheth at the shaking of a spear." What can a man do in this case? If a man could have Job's horse, and had skill and courage to ride him, he might do notable things. "For his neck is clothed with thunder, he will not be afraid of the grasshopper, the glory of his nostrils is terrible, he paweth in the valley, rejoiceth in his strength, and goeth out to meet the armed men. He mocketh at fear, and is not affrighted, neither turneth back from the sword. The quiver rattleth against him, the glittering spear, and the shield. He swalloweth the ground with fierceness and rage, neither believeth he that is the sound of the trumpet. He saith among the trumpets, Ha, ha! and he smelleth the battle afar off, the thundering of the captains, and the shoutings."

But for such travelers as you and I, let us never desire to meet with an enemy, nor brag as if we could do better when we hear of others who have been defeated, nor be delighted by thoughts of our own bravery; for those who do usually come out the worst when they are tried. Look at Peter, whom I mentioned before. He boasted, yes, he did, saying that he would do better and stand more firmly for his Master than all other men; but who was more defeated by these villains than he?

Therefore when we hear of such robberies on the King's highway, there are two things we should do:

1. Go out clad in armor, and be sure to take a shield with us; for it was for lack of that, that he who attacked Leviathan could not make him yield: for indeed, he does not fear us at all if we are without armor and shield. Therefore he who has skill has said, "Above all take the shield of faith, wherewith ye shall be able to quench all the fiery darts of the wicked."

2. We should also ask the King for a protective escort; yes, we should ask that he go with us himself. This made David rejoice when he was in the Valley of the Shadow of Death; and Moses would rather have died where he stood than go one step without his God. Oh, my brother, if he goes with us, why should we be afraid of ten thousand who set themselves against us? But without him, the proud helpers "fall under the slain."

For my part, I have been in the battle before; and though, through his goodness, I am alive, I cannot boast of my own bravery. I shall be glad if I encounter no more of such attacks, but I fear we are not beyond all danger. However, since the lion and the bear have not as yet devoured me, I hope God will also deliver us from the next uncircumcised Philistine. Then sang Christian:

> *Poor Little-faith! Hast been among the thieves?*
> *Wast robbed? Remember this, whoso believes*
> *And gets more faith; shall then a victor be*
> *Over ten thousand, else scarce over three.*

So they went on, with Ignorance following, until they came to a place where another pathway joined their way, and it seemed to lie as straight as the way they should go; and they did not know which of the two paths to take, for both seemed to lie straight before them. Therefore they stopped to decide what to do. And as they were thinking about the way, a black man dressed in a very light robe came to them and asked them why they were standing there. They told him they were going to the Celestial City, but did not know which way to go. "Follow me," said the man, "for that is where I am going." So they followed him down the path that had just intersected with the road, which gradually turned, and turned them so far that soon their faces were turned away from the city to which they desired to go. Still, they followed him. But by and by, before they realized it, he had led them both into a net, in which they became so entangled that they didn't know what to do; and with that the white robe fell off the black man's back and they saw where they were. Then they lay there crying for some time because they could not free themselves.

CHRISTIAN: Now I see my error. Didn't the Shepherds tell us to beware of the flatterers? As the wise man says, "A man that flattereth his neighbor spreadeth a net for his feet."

HOPEFUL: They also gave us a map of the way, but we have forgotten to read it and have not kept ourselves from the paths of the destroyer. Here David was wiser than we, for he said, "Concerning the works of men, by the word of thy lips, I have kept me from the paths of the destroyer."

Thus they lay sorrowing in the net, until at last they noticed a Shining One coming toward them with a whip of small cord in his hand. When he reached them, he asked where they came from and what they were doing there. They told him they were poor pilgrims going to Zion, but had been led astray by a black man dressed in white. "He told us to follow him," they said, "for he was going there too." Then the man with the whip said, "It was Flatterer, a false apostle, who has transformed himself into an angel of light." So he tore open the net and released the men. Then he said to them, "Follow me so that I may set you on your way again." So he led them back to the pathway they had left to follow the Flatterer. Then he asked them, "Where did you stay last night?" They said, "With the

Shepherds, upon the Delectable Mountains." Then he asked them if those Shepherds had given them a map of the way. They answered, "Yes." "When you were at a standstill," said he, "did you take out your map and read it?" They answered, "No." He asked them, "Why?" They said, "We forgot." Then he asked them if the Shepherds had warned them to beware of the Flatterer. They answered, "Yes, but we never imagined that this fine-spoken man was he."

Then I saw in my dream that he commanded them to lie down; and when they did, he chastised them severely to teach them that they should walk in the good way; and as he chastised them, he said, "As many as I love, I rebuke and chasten; be zealous, therefore, and repent." This done, he told them to go on their way and to heed carefully the other directions of the Shepherds. So they thanked him for all his kindness and went softly along the right way, singing:

> Come hither, you that walk along the way;
> See how the pilgrims fare that go astray!
> They catched are in an entangling net,
> 'Cause they good counsel lightly did forget:
> 'Tis true they rescued were, but yet you see,
> They're scourged to boot.
> Let this your caution be.

Now after a while they saw someone in the distance, walking leisurely and alone along the highway. Then said Christian to his companion, "Yonder is a man with his back toward Zion, and he is coming to meet us."

HOPEFUL: I see him. Let us be careful now, lest he should prove to be another flatterer.

The man came closer and closer, until at last he came up to them. His name was Atheist, and he asked them where they were going.

CHRISTIAN: We are going to Mount Zion.

Then Atheist began to laugh loudly.

CHRISTIAN: What is the meaning of your laughter?

ATHEIST: I am laughing because I see what ignorant people you are, to make such a tedious journey, when you will probably have nothing but your travel to show for your effort.

CHRISTIAN: Why, man, do you think we shall not be received?

ATHEIST: Received! The place you dream about does not exist anywhere in the world.

CHRISTIAN: But it does in the world to come.

ATHEIST: When I was at home in my own country, I heard about this place, and after hearing about it, I went out to see it. I have been seeking this city for twenty years, and know no more about it than I did the first day I set out.

CHRISTIAN: We have both heard that there is such a place, and we believe it may be found.

ATHEIST: If I had not believed, when I was still at home, I would not have come this far to seek it; but finding nothing (and I should have if there were such a place to be found, for I have gone further than you to seek it), I am going back again, and will seek to refresh myself with the things that I then cast away for hopes of that which I now see is not.

Then Christian said to Hopeful, "Is what this man says true?"

HOPEFUL: Be careful; he is one of the flatterers. Remember what listening to such a fellow has cost us already. No Mount Zion!? Why, did we not see the gate of the city from the Delectable Mountains? And besides, are we not to walk by faith?

Let us move on, lest the man with the whip overtake us again. You should have taught me that which I will whisper in your ear: "Cease, my son, to hear the instruction that causeth to err from the words of knowledge." Stop listening to him, and let us "believe to the saving of the soul."

CHRISTIAN: My brother, I did not put the question to you because I doubted the truth of what we believe, but to test you and draw from you what you honestly think in your heart. As for this man, I know he is blinded by the god of this world. So let us go on, knowing that what we believe is the truth, and that no lie comes from the truth.

HOPEFUL: Now I "rejoice in hope of the glory of God."

So they turned away from the man. And he, laughing at them, went his way.

I saw then in my dream that they walked until they entered a country where the air tended to make strangers drowsy. And here Hopeful began to feel listless and sleepy, and he said to Christian, "I feel so sleepy that I can hardly keep my eyes open. Let's lie down here and take a nap."

CHRISTIAN: No, we cannot, for if we sleep here, we may never wake up again.

HOPEFUL: Why, my brother? Sleep is sweet to the working man. We will be refreshed if we take a nap.

CHRISTIAN: Do you not remember that one of the Shepherds told us to beware of the Enchanted Ground? By that, he meant that we should beware of sleeping. Therefore, "let us not sleep, as do others, but let us watch and be sober."

HOPEFUL: I acknowledge my weakness, and had I been here alone, I would have risked the danger of death by sleeping. I see that what the wise man says is true: "Two are better than one." Up to this time, your company has been a fortunate circumstance for me, "and you shall have a good reward for your labor."

CHRISTIAN: Now then, to keep from getting drowsy in this place, let's have some good discussion.

HOPEFUL: I agree wholeheartedly.

CHRISTIAN: Where shall we begin?

HOPEFUL: Where God began with us. But you begin, if you please.

CHRISTIAN: First I will sing you this song:

When saints do sleepy grow, let them come hither,
And hear how these two pilgrims talk together:
Yea, let them learn of them, in any wise,
Thus to keep ope their drowsy slumbering eyes.
Saints' fellowship, if it be managed well,
Keeps them awake, and that in spite of hell.

Then Christian began and said, "I will ask you a question. Why did you first think of doing what you are doing now?"

HOPEFUL: Do you mean, why did I begin to be concerned about my soul?

CHRISTIAN: Yes, that is what I mean.

HOPEFUL: For a long time I enjoyed those things that were seen and sold at our fair; things that, I believe now, would have (had I continued in them) destroyed me.

CHRISTIAN: What things?

HOPEFUL: All the treasures and riches of the world. I also delighted in debauchery, partying, drinking, swearing, lying, immorality, Sabbath-breaking, and every other thing that tends to destroy the soul. But by hearing and considering divine things, which I learned about from you, as well as from beloved Faithful who was put to death at Vanity Fair for his faith and goodness, I discovered at last that "the end of these things is death." And that for these things "the wrath of God cometh upon the children of disobedience."

CHRISTIAN: Did you immediately come under conviction?

HOPEFUL: No, for I was not willing at first to recognize the evil of sin or the damnation that results from it; instead, when my mind was initially shaken by the Word, I tried to shut my eyes against the light.

CHRISTIAN: But what caused you to maintain this attitude before God's blessed Spirit began working upon you?

HOPEFUL: Well, first, I did not know that this was the work of God upon me. I never realized that God begins the conversion of a sinner by first awakening him to sin. Second, sin was still very enjoyable to me, and I didn't want to leave it. Third, I did not know how to part with my old companions, for their presence and their actions were so desirable to me. And fourth, the times when I was under conviction were such troubling and frightening hours that I could not bear even the memories of them.

CHRISTIAN: Then, there were times when you were not troubled?

HOPEFUL: Oh, yes, but then it would haunt me again, and I was as bad, no, worse, than before.

CHRISTIAN: What was it that brought your sins to mind again?

HOPEFUL: Many things, such as,

1. If I met a good man on the streets; or,

2. If I heard anyone read the Bible; or,

3. If my head began to ache; or,

4. If I was told that some of my neighbors were sick; or,

5. If I heard the bell toll for someone who had died; or,

6. If I thought of dying myself; or,

7. If I heard that someone else had died suddenly,

8. But especially when I thought of myself and that I must soon face judgment.

CHRISTIAN: And could you ever easily get rid of the guilt of sin when any of these occurrences brought it upon you?

HOPEFUL: No, I could not, for they were gaining a greater hold on my conscience; and if I even thought about returning to sin (though my mind was turned against it), it was doubly tormenting to me.

CHRISTIAN: And what did you do then?

HOPEFUL: I thought I must try to change my life; otherwise, I thought, I would surely be damned.

CHRISTIAN: And did you try to change?

HOPEFUL: Yes. I tried not to sin, and I avoided sinful company; I began performing religious duties such as prayer, Bible reading, weeping over my sins, speaking the truth to my neighbors, and so forth. These things I did, along with many others, too numerous to relate.

CHRISTIAN: And did you then think you were all right?

HOPEFUL: Yes, for a while. But then my trouble came tumbling upon me again, despite all my changes.

CHRISTIAN: How did that come about, since you had now reformed?

HOPEFUL: Several things brought it upon me, especially such sayings as these: "All our righteousnesses are as filthy rags." "By the works of the law no man shall be justified." "When you have done all things, say, We are unprofitable"; and many more like this. From there I began to reason with myself: If all my righteousnesses are like filthy rags; if no man can be justified by obeying the law; and if, when we have done all we can, we are still unworthy, then it is foolish to think we can get to heaven by the law. Furthermore, I thought: If a man runs up a bill of a hundred pounds with a shopkeeper, and after that he pays for everything he buys but still owes his old bill, the shopkeeper can still sue him and send him to prison until he pays the debt.

CHRISTIAN: How did you apply this to yourself?

HOPEFUL: Why, I thought, I have by my sins run up a great charge in God's book, and my reforming now will not pay off that debt. Therefore, I should continue with my present changes; but how shall I be freed from the damnation I have brought upon myself by my former transgressions?

CHRISTIAN: A very good application. But please continue.

HOPEFUL: Another thing that has troubled me, even since the recent changes in my life, is that if I look carefully at the best of what I do now, I still see sin, new sin, mixing itself with the best of what I do; so I am forced to conclude that, even if my former life had been faultless, I have now committed sin enough in one action to send me to hell.

CHRISTIAN: And what did you do then?

HOPEFUL: Do! I did not know what to do, until I shared my thoughts with Faithful, for he and I were well acquainted. And he told me that unless I could obtain the righteousness of a man who had never sinned, neither my own nor all the righteousness of the world could save me.

CHRISTIAN: And did you think he spoke the truth?

HOPEFUL: Had he told me this when I was pleased and satisfied with my own improvements, I would have called him a fool; but now, since I saw my own frailty and the sin that clung to even my best performance, I was forced to accept his opinion.

CHRISTIAN: But did you think, when he first suggested it to you, that a man could be found, of whom it could justly be said, "He never committed any sin"?

HOPEFUL: I must confess the words sounded strange at first, but after we talked more and I spent more time in his company, I was totally convinced of it.

CHRISTIAN: And did you ask him who this man was and how you could be justified by him?

HOPEFUL: Yes, and he told me it was the Lord Jesus, who dwells at the right hand of the Most High. "You must be justified by him, by trusting in what he alone has done during his life on earth and his suffering on the cross." I asked him how that man's righteousness could justify another before God. And he told me that the man was the mighty God, and that he had done what he did and died on the cross not for himself, but for me; and if I believed on him, his righteousness would be applied to my account.

CHRISTIAN: And what did you do then?

HOPEFUL: I stated my objections against my believing this, because I didn't think the Lord was willing to save me.

CHRISTIAN: What did Faithful say to you then?

HOPEFUL: He told me to go to Christ and see. I said I thought that was presumptive. But he said, no, it was not, for I was invited to come. Then he gave me a book of Jesus, his authoritative Word, to encourage me to come freely; and he said that every jot and tittle of that book stands firmer than heaven and earth. Then I asked him what I must do when I came to him; and he told me I must kneel down and plead with all my heart and soul for the Father to reveal him to me. Then I asked Faithful how I should approach him, and he said, "Go, and you shall find him upon a mercy-seat, where he sits all year long, to give pardon and forgiveness to those who come to him." I told him that I did not know what to say when I came. And he told me to say, in effect: God be merciful to me a sinner, and help me to know and believe in Jesus Christ; for I see that without his righteousness, and my faith in that righteousness, I am utterly lost. Lord, I have heard that you are a merciful God and have sent your Son Jesus Christ to be the Savior of the world; and moreover, that you are willing to bestow him upon such a poor sinner as I am (and I am a sinner indeed); Lord, take therefore this opportunity, and magnify your grace in the salvation of my soul, through your Son Jesus Christ. Amen.

CHRISTIAN: And did you do as you were told?

HOPEFUL: Yes, over and over and over.

CHRISTIAN: And did the Father reveal his Son to you?

HOPEFUL: Not at the first, nor the second, nor the third, nor the fourth, nor the fifth; no, nor at the sixth time.

CHRISTIAN: What did you do then?

HOPEFUL: Why, I could not tell what to do!

CHRISTIAN: Did you think of not praying anymore?

HOPEFUL: Yes, a hundred times over.

CHRISTIAN: So why didn't you stop?

HOPEFUL: I believed that what I had been told was true; that is, that without the righteousness of this Christ, all the world could not save me; and therefore I thought that if I quit praying, I would die, so I will die at the throne of grace. And with that, this came to my mind: "If it tarry, wait for it; because it will surely come, it will not tarry." So I continued praying until the Father showed me his Son.

CHRISTIAN: And how was he revealed to you?

HOPEFUL: I did not see him with my earthly eyes, but with the eyes of my understanding; and this is how it was: One day I was very sad, sadder than at any other time in my life, and this sorrow was the result of a fresh glimpse of the magnitude and vileness of my sins. And as I sat there expecting nothing but hell and the everlasting damnation of my soul, suddenly I saw the Lord Jesus Christ look down from heaven at me and say, "Believe on the Lord Jesus Christ, and thou shalt be saved."

But I replied, "Lord, I am a great, a very great sinner." And he answered, "My grace is sufficient for thee." Then I said, "But, Lord, what is believing?" And then, from the verse, "He that cometh to me shall never hunger, and he that believeth on me shall never thirst," I recognized that believing and coming were the same thing; and that he who sought after salvation through Christ with his whole heart, he indeed believed in Christ. Then tears came to my eyes, and I asked, "But, Lord, can such a great sinner as I really be accepted by you and saved by you?" And I heard him say, "Him that cometh to me, I will in no wise cast out." Then I said, "But, Lord, how should I think of you when coming to you, so that my faith is in you?" Then he said, "Christ Jesus came into the world to save sinners." "He is the end of the law for righteousness to every one that believes." "He died for our sins, and rose again for our justification: he loved us, and washed us from our sins in his own blood." "He is mediator between God and us." "He ever liveth to make intercession for us." And I gathered from all of these Scriptures that I must look for righteousness in his person and for satisfaction for my sins through his blood; that what he did in obedience to his Father's law, submitting to its penalty, was not for himself, but for anyone who will accept it for his salvation and be thankful. And now my heart was filled with joy, my eyes filled with tears, and my heart brimming over with love for the name, people, and ways of Jesus Christ.

CHRISTIAN: This indeed was a revelation of Christ to your soul. But tell me, what effect did this have upon your spirit?

HOPEFUL: It made me see that all the world, regardless of any good it might contain, is in a state of condemnation. It made me see that God the Father, though he is just, can justify the sinner who comes to him. It made me greatly ashamed of the vileness of my former life, and dismayed me with the sense of my own ignorance; for before now, nothing had so clearly showed me the beauty of Jesus Christ. It made me love a holy life and long to do something for the honor and glory of the name of the Lord Jesus; yes, had I now a thousand gallons of blood in my body, I would have shed it all for the sake of the Lord Jesus.

I saw then in my dream that Hopeful looked back and saw Ignorance, whom they had left behind. "Look," he said to Christian, "how that youngster lingers far behind."

CHRISTIAN: Yes, yes, I see him. He doesn't care for our company.

HOPEFUL: But it wouldn't have hurt him to have kept up with us.

CHRISTIAN: That's true, but I guarantee you he thinks otherwise.

HOPEFUL: That, I think, he does; however, let's wait for him. So they did.

Then Christian said to him, "Come on, man, why do you stay so far behind?"

IGNORANCE: I enjoy walking alone, unless I particularly like the company.

Then Christian said softly to Hopeful, "Didn't I tell you he doesn't care for our company? But let's pass the time in this desolate place by talking to him." Then he turned to Ignorance and said, "How are you? And how do things stand between God and your soul now?"

IGNORANCE: Well I hope; for I am filled with good notions that come to mind and comfort me as I walk.

CHRISTIAN: What good notions? Please tell us.

IGNORANCE: Why, I think of God and heaven.

CHRISTIAN: So do the devils and damned souls.

IGNORANCE: But I think of them and desire them.

CHRISTIAN: So do many that are never likely to get there. "The soul of the sluggard desireth, and hath nothing."

IGNORANCE: But I think of them and leave all for them.

CHRISTIAN: That I doubt; for leaving all is a hard thing to do—harder than many realize. But what makes you think you have left all for God and heaven?

IGNORANCE: My heart tells me so.

CHRISTIAN: The wise man says, "He that trusts his own heart is a fool."

IGNORANCE: That applies to an evil heart, but mine is good.

CHRISTIAN: But how do you prove that?

IGNORANCE: Because it comforts me with the hope of heaven.

CHRISTIAN: That may be through its own deceitfulness; for a man's heart may comfort him with hopes of that thing for which he has no grounds to hope.

IGNORANCE: But my heart and life agree, and therefore my hope is well grounded.

CHRISTIAN: Who told you that your heart and life agree?

IGNORANCE: My heart tells me so.

CHRISTIAN: Ask my friend here if I am a thief! Your heart tells you so! Unless the Word of God bears witness to this matter, other testimony is of no value.

IGNORANCE: But is it not a good heart that has good thoughts? And is not that a good life that is in accordance with God's commandments?

CHRISTIAN: Yes, it is a good heart that has good thoughts, and it is a good life that is in accordance with God's commandments; but it is one thing indeed to have these, and another thing only to think so.

IGNORANCE: Please tell me, what do you consider good thoughts and a life in accordance with God's commandments?

CHRISTIAN: There are good thoughts of various kinds; some regarding ourselves, some God, some Christ, and some other things.

IGNORANCE: What would be good thoughts regarding ourselves?

CHRISTIAN: Those that agree with the Word of God.

IGNORANCE: When do our thoughts about ourselves agree with the Word of God?

CHRISTIAN: When we pass the same judgment upon ourselves which the Word passes. To explain what I mean: The Word of God says of the natural man, "There is none righteous, there is none that doeth good." It says also that "every imagination of the heart of man is only evil, and that continually." And again, "The imagination of man's heart is evil from his youth." Now then, when we think thus of ourselves, having a real sense of it, then our thoughts are good ones, because they are in agreement with the Word of God.

IGNORANCE: I will never believe that my heart is that bad.

CHRISTIAN: Therefore you have never had one good thought concerning yourself in your entire life. But let me go on. As the Word passes a judgment upon our hearts, so it passes a judgment upon our ways; and when OUR hearts and OUR ways agree with the judgment which the Word gives on both, then both are good, because they agree with it.

IGNORANCE: Explain what you mean.

CHRISTIAN: Why, the Word of God says that man's ways are crooked ways, not good, but corrupt. It says they are naturally out of the good way, and they do not know it. Now when a man thinks this about his ways, both realistically and with humility, then he has good thoughts about his own ways, because his thoughts now agree with the judgment of the Word of God.

IGNORANCE: What are good thoughts concerning God?

CHRISTIAN: Just as I have said concerning ourselves, when our thoughts about God agree with what the Word says about him; and that is, when we think of his being and attributes as the Word teaches; which I cannot right now discuss at length. But to speak of him with reference to us: We have right thoughts about God when we think that he knows us better than we know ourselves, and can see sin in us when and where we see none in ourselves; when we think he knows our innermost thoughts, and when our hearts are always open to his eyes; and when we think that all our righteousness stinks in his nostrils, and that therefore He cannot bear to see us stand before Him with any confidence, even in our best performances.

IGNORANCE: Do you think I am such a fool as to think God can see no further than I can or that I would come to God in the best of my performances?

CHRISTIAN: So what do you think about this matter?

IGNORANCE: Why, to be brief, I think I must believe in Christ for justification.

CHRISTIAN: What? You think you must believe in Christ when you don't see your need of him! You see neither your original sin nor your actual sin, but have such an opinion of yourself, and of what you do, that you are clearly revealed as one who has never seen a necessity for Christ's personal righteousness to justify you before God. How then can you say, "I believe in Christ"?

IGNORANCE: I believe well enough.

CHRISTIAN: What do you believe?

IGNORANCE: I believe that Christ died for sinners, and that I shall be justified before God through his gracious acceptance of my obedience to his law. Christ makes my religious works acceptable to his Father by virtue of his merits, and thus I shall be justified.

CHRISTIAN: Let me give this response to your confession of faith:

1. You believe with an imaginary faith, for this faith is described nowhere in the Word.

2. You believe with a false faith, because it takes justification from the personal righteousness of Christ and applies it to your own.

3. This faith makes Christ a justifier of your works, not of your person, and for your works' sake, which is false.

4. Therefore, this faith is deceptive and will leave you under the wrath of God Almighty in the day of judgment; for true justifying faith sends the soul (aware of its lost condition by the law) flying for refuge to Christ's righteousness. And his righteousness is not an act of grace by which he makes your obedience acceptable to God as a justification; but it is his personal obedience to the law in doing and suffering for us that which would be required of us. This is the righteousness that true

faith accepts, and under which the soul is covered and presented as spotless before God, and acquitted of condemnation.

IGNORANCE: What! Would you have us trust in what Christ in his own person has done without us? This kind of thinking would free us to live however we liked. For why would it matter how we live, if all we have to do is believe we can be justified by Christ's personal righteousness?

CHRISTIAN: Ignorance is your name, and so are you; even this answer demonstrates it. You are ignorant of what justifying righteousness is, and you are ignorant of how to save your soul from the wrath of God through faith in that righteousness. Yes, you also are ignorant of the true effects of saving faith in this righteousness of Christ, which means to yield the heart to God in Christ, to love his name, his Word, his ways, and his people.

HOPEFUL: Ask him if he ever had Christ revealed to him from heaven.

IGNORANCE: What! You believe in revelations! I think that what you and all the rest say about that matter is just the result of disordered minds.

HOPEFUL: Why, man! Christ is so hidden in God from our natural understanding that he cannot be known by any man unless God the Father reveals him to us.

IGNORANCE: That is your faith, but not mine. Yet I have no doubt that mine is as good as yours.

CHRISTIAN: Allow me to interject this word: You should not speak so lightly of this matter. For this I will boldly affirm (even as my good friend has done), that no man can know Jesus Christ except by the revelation of the Father: yes, and faith too, by which the soul lays hold upon Christ, must be formed by his mighty power; of which, poor Ignorance, you are ignorant.

So wake up! See your own wretchedness, and fly to the Lord Jesus; and by his righteousness, which is the righteousness of God (for he himself is God), you shall be delivered from condemnation.

IGNORANCE: You go so fast, I cannot keep up with you. You go on ahead; I must stay behind for a while.

Then they said:

> *Well, Ignorance, wilt thou yet foolish be,*
> *To slight good counsel, ten times given thee?*
> *And if thou yet refuse it, you shalt know*
> *Ere long the evil of thy doing so.*
>
> *Remember, man, in time; stoop, do not fear,*
> *Good counsel taken well, saves: therefore hear.*
> *But if thou yet shalt slight it, thou wilt be*
> *The loser, Ignorance, I'll warrant thee.*

Then Christian said to his friend and companion, "Well, come, my good Hopeful, I see that you and I must walk by ourselves again."

So I saw in my dream that Christian and Hopeful walked on quickly, while Ignorance came hobbling behind. Then said Christian to his companion, "I pity this poor man, for he will certainly have a hard time at the end."

HOPEFUL: Sadly, there are many in our town in the same condition; whole families, yes, whole streets, and some are pilgrims too. And if there are that many in our part of the world, how many must there be in the place where he was born?

CHRISTIAN: Indeed the Word says, "He hath blinded their eyes lest they should see." But now that we are by ourselves, tell me, what do you think of such men? Have they never been convicted of sin and consequently have no fears about the dangerous conditions of their souls?

HOPEFUL: You tell me what you think, for you are the elder.

CHRISTIAN: I think that sometimes they may come under conviction, but being naturally ignorant, they do not understand that such convictions are for their good; and therefore they desperately seek to stifle them, and continue to flatter themselves that their own hearts are right.

HOPEFUL: I believe, as you say, that fear often works for men's own good when they begin to go on pilgrimage.

CHRISTIAN: Without any doubt it does, if it is the right kind of fear; for the Word says, "The fear of the Lord is the beginning of wisdom."

HOPEFUL: How would you describe the right kind of fear?

CHRISTIAN: True or right fear can be discerned by three things:

1. By its origin: it is caused by the conviction that one needs salvation for sin.

2. It drives the soul to cling to Christ for salvation.

3. It creates within the soul a great reverence for God, His Word, and His ways, keeping the soul sensitive to all of these and making it afraid to turn from them, to the right hand or to the left, to anything that might dishonor God, destroy the soul's peace, or grieve the Spirit.

HOPEFUL: I believe you have spoken the truth. Are we almost past the Enchanted Ground now?

CHRISTIAN: Why? Are you weary of this conversation?

HOPEFUL: No, not at all, but I would like to know where we are.

CHRISTIAN: We have no more than two miles to go. But let us return to the matter we were discussing. Now the ignorant do not know that convictions that tend to make them fearful are for their good, and therefore they seek to stifle them.

HOPEFUL: How do they do this?

CHRISTIAN:

1. They think those fears are the work of the devil (though indeed they are caused by God), so they resist them as though they are things that will lead to their defeat.

2. They also think these fears tend to spoil their faith, when, sadly enough, they have no faith at all! And so they harden their hearts against these fears.

3. They assume they ought not to fear, and therefore, in spite of the fears, they grow presumptuously self-confident.

4. They see that those fears tend to destroy their pitiful self-righteousness, and they resist them with all their might.

HOPEFUL: I know something about this myself, for that is the way I used to be.

CHRISTIAN: Well, we will leave our neighbor Ignorance by himself for now and find another worthwhile question to discuss.

HOPEFUL: I agree totally, but you shall still begin.

CHRISTIAN: Well then, were you acquainted with a fellow named Temporary, who lived in your area about ten years ago and was opposed to religion?

HOPEFUL: Know him! Yes indeed. He lived in Graceless, a town about two miles from Honesty, and he lived next door to Turnback.

CHRISTIAN: Right. Actually they lived under the same roof. Well, at one point I believe that man had some awareness of and insight into his sinful state and the punishment it deserved.

HOPEFUL: I think the same thing, for my house was no more than three miles from his, and he would often come to me in tears. Truly I pitied the man, and was not altogether without hope for him. But from this one may see that not everyone who cries, "Lord, Lord," will enter the way.

CHRISTIAN: He told me once that he was resolved to go on pilgrimage, as we are now; but all of a sudden he made the acquaintance of Save-self, and then he became a stranger to me.

HOPEFUL: Since we are talking about him, let us investigate the reason for his sudden backsliding, and that of others like him.

CHRISTIAN: That could be very profitable. Why don't you begin?

HOPEFUL: Well, in my judgment there are four reasons for it:

1. Though the consciences of such men are awakened, their minds are not changed; therefore, when the guilt passes, they cease

to be religious. They return to their old ways again, just as the dog returns to its vomit. Thus they are eager for heaven only because they fear the torments of hell; and as soon as their sense of hell and their fears of damnation chill and cool, so does their desire for heaven and salvation. When their guilt and fears are gone, their desires for heaven and happiness die, and they return to their old course again.

2. Another reason is that they are slaves to certain fears that overpower them; particularly the fear of men, for "the fear of men bringeth a snare." So although they seem eager for heaven as long as the flames of hell are about their ears, when that terror abates, they begin to have second thoughts: namely, that it is good to be wise and not run the risk of losing all, or at least not bringing themselves unnecessary trouble. And so they fall in with the world again.

3. The stigma that surrounds religion is also a stumbling block to them. They are high and mighty, and they consider religion low and common; therefore, when they have lost their sense of hell and the wrath to come, they return to their former ways.

4. They do not even like to think about guilt and fear, or the possibility of future misery; if they did, perhaps the foresight might make them flee to where the righteous flee and are safe. But because they shun even the thoughts of guilt and fear, when once they are rid of their awakenings about the terrors and wrath of God, they gladly harden their hearts and choose ways that will harden them more and more.

CHRISTIAN: You are near the truth, for at the bottom of it all is the need for change in mind and will. They are like the felon who stands before the judge: he shakes and trembles and seems to repent; but at the bottom of it all is his fear of punishment, not any regret for his crime. Let this man have his freedom, and he will still be a thief and a scoundrel, whereas if his mind were changed, he would be otherwise.

HOPEFUL: I have pointed out the reasons for their backsliding; now you tell me how it happens.

CHRISTIAN: So I will, willingly.

1. As much as they can, they turn their thoughts away from any reminder of God, death, and judgment to come.

2. Then they gradually cease their private duties, such as devotional prayer, curbing their lusts, being vigilant, being repentant for sin, and the like.

3. Then they shun the company of lively and sincere Christians.

4. After that they grow indifferent to public duties such as hearing and reading the Word, gathering together for worship, and the like.

5. Then they begin to find fault with some of the godly, and the devilish purpose behind this is to find some alleged reason for turning away from religion.

6. Then they begin to associate with worldly, immoral, and sensual men.

7. Then they secretly indulge in worldly and lewd conversations; and they are happy if they can find any who are considered honest doing the same, so they may use their example as an excuse to indulge more boldly.

8. After this they begin to play with little sins openly.

9. And then, being hardened, they show themselves as they really are. Launched again into the gulf of misery, they are lost forever in their own deception, unless a miracle of grace prevents it.

Now I saw in my dream that by this time the pilgrims had crossed the Enchanted Ground and entered the country of Beulah, where the air was very sweet and pleasant; the pathway lay directly through it, and they found comfort and restoration there for a time. In this land the flowers bloomed every day, and the pilgrims continually heard the singing of birds and the voice of the turtledove in the land. Here the sun shone night and day, for this was beyond the Valley of the Shadow of Death and out of the reach of Giant Despair; in fact, they could not even see Doubting Castle from this place. Here they were within sight of the city to which they were going, and here they met some of the inhabitants of that place; for the Shining Ones frequently walked in this land, because it was upon the borders of heaven. In this land also the contract between the bride and the bridegroom was renewed; yes, here, "As the bridegroom rejoiceth over the bride, so did their God rejoice over them." Here they had no lack of corn and wine; for in this place they found an abundance of that which they had sought during all their pilgrimage. Here they heard voices from the Celestial City, loud voices, saying, "Say ye to the daughter of Zion, Behold, thy salvation cometh! Behold, his reward is with him." Here all the inhabitants of the country called them "the holy people, the redeemed of the Lord, sought out."

As they walked in this land, they rejoiced more than they had in those places that were more remote from the kingdom to which they were going; and as they drew near to the city, they had a more perfect view of it. It was built of pearls and precious stones, and the street was paved with gold; and the natural glory of the city and the reflection of the sunbeams upon it made Christian sick with desire; Hopeful also had a spell or two of the same disease. Because of this, they lay down for a while, crying out, "If you see my beloved, tell him I am sick of love."

Then, when they had gained a little strength and were able to bear their sickness, they walked on, getting closer and closer to the city, where there were orchards, vineyards, and gardens, and their gates opened onto the highway. As they came up to these places, they noticed the gardener standing in the path, and they asked him, "Whose vineyards and gardens are these?" He answered, "They are the King's, and are planted here for his own enjoyment and for the consolation of pilgrims."

So the gardener led them into the vineyards and told them to refresh themselves with the delicious fruit. He also showed them where the King walked and where his favorite arbors were; and here they stopped and slept.

Now I noticed in my dream that they talked more in their sleep at this time than they ever had during the rest of their journey; and as I was wondering about this, the gardener said even to me, "Why are you marveling at this? The fruit of the grapes of these vineyards goes down so sweetly that it causes the lips of those who are asleep to speak."

Then I saw that when they awoke, they prepared themselves to go up to the city. But, as I said, the reflection of the sun upon the city (for "the city was pure gold") was so glorious that they could not look at it directly, but had to view it through an instrument made for that purpose. As they went on, they were met by two men in garments that shone like gold; also their faces shone like light.

These men asked the pilgrims where they had come from, and Christian and Hopeful told them. They also asked them where they had lodged, and what difficulties and dangers, what comforts and pleasures they had encountered on the way, and Christian and Hopeful told them. Then the men said, "You have only two more difficulties to deal with, and then you will be in the city."

Christian and his companion asked the men to go along with them; so they told them they would. "But," they said, "you must reach the city by your own faith." So I saw in my dream that they went on together until they came within sight of the gate.

Now I noticed that between them and the gate was a river, but there was no bridge across it, and the river was very deep. At the sight of this river, the pilgrims were stunned; but the men who were with them said, "You must go through, or you cannot get to the gate."

The pilgrims then asked whether there was any other way to get to the gate, to which the men answered, "Yes, but since the foundation of the world, only two, Enoch and Elijah, have ever been permitted to take that path, and that shall be the case until the last trumpet sounds." The pilgrims then, especially Christian, began to despair, looking this way and that; but they could find no way by which they might escape the river. Then they asked the men if the waters were all the same depth. They said, "No," but they could not help them with that either, "for," they said, "you will find it deeper or shallower, according to your faith in the King of the place."

They then waded into the water, and Christian began to sink, crying out to his good friend Hopeful, "I sink in deep waters; the billows go over my head, all his waves go over me! Selah."

Then Hopeful said, "Have courage, my brother, for I feel the bottom, and it is solid." Then said Christian, "Ah! my friend, the sorrows of death surround me; I shall not see the land that flows with milk and honey."

And with that a great darkness and horror fell upon Christian so that he could not see before him. Also he became so distraught that he could neither remember, nor speak reasonably about those blessings he had encountered on his pilgrimage. Everything he said focused on his terrible fears of heart and mind and that he should die in that river and never enter the gate. He was also greatly troubled with thoughts about the sins he had committed, both since and before he began to be a pilgrim. Also, his words revealed that he was troubled by visions of demons and evil spirits.

Hopeful therefore had all he could do to keep his brother's head above water; in fact, at times Christian almost disappeared, only to rise up again half dead. Hopeful also tried to comfort him, saying, "Brother, I see the gate, and there are men waiting to receive us." But Christian would answer, "It is you, it is you they wait for; you have been hopeful ever since I knew you." "And so have you," said Hopeful to Christian. "Ah! brother!" he said, "surely if I was right he would now come to help me; but because of my sins he has led me into this trap and deserted me."

Then said Hopeful, "My brother, you have forgotten the text where it is said of the wicked, 'There is no band in their death, but their strength is firm. They are not troubled as other men, neither are they plagued like other men.'" These troubles you are going through in these waters are not a sign that God has forsaken you, but are sent to try you, testing whether you will remember all his previous mercy to you and rely upon him in your distress.

Then I saw in my dream that Christian seemed to be in deep thought for a while, during which Hopeful added, "Be of good cheer, Jesus Christ maketh thee whole." And with that Christian cried out with a loud voice, "Oh! I see him again, and he tells me, 'When thou passest through the waters, I will be with thee; and through the rivers, they shall not overflow thee.'"

Then they both took courage, and after that the enemy was as silent as a stone, until they had crossed over. Presently Christian found ground to stand upon, and then the rest of the river was shallow. Thus they crossed over.

Now on the bank of the river on the other side they saw the two Shining Men again, waiting for them. "We are ministering spirits," they said, "sent to minister to those who are heirs of salvation." And thus they went along toward the gate.

Now the city stood upon a great hill, but the pilgrims climbed that hill with ease because they had these two men to lead them and to lean upon; also they had left their mortal garments behind them in the river. Therefore they went up with much agility and speed, though the foundation upon which the city rested was higher than the clouds. They climbed up through the air, talking happily as they went, comforted because they had safely crossed the river and had such glorious companions to accompany them.

> *Now, now look how the holy pilgrims ride,*
> *Clouds are their chariots, angels are their guide:*
> *Who would not here for him all hazards run,*
> *That thus provides for his when this world's done?*

They talked about the magnificence of the place with the Shining Ones, who told them that the beauty and glory of it was inexpressible. "There," they said, "is Mount Zion, the heavenly Jerusalem, the company of angels, and the spirits of just men made perfect. You are going now to the paradise of God, where you will see the tree of life and eat of its never-fading fruits; and there you will have white robes given you, and you will walk and talk every day with the King, all the days of eternity. There you will never again see such things as you saw when you were upon the earth, such as sorrow, sickness, affliction, and death, 'for the former things are passed away.' You are now going to Abraham, to Isaac, and Jacob, and to the prophets—men whom God has 'taken away from the evil to come,' and who are now resting upon their beds, each one walking in his righteousness."

Christian and Hopeful then asked, "What shall we do in the holy place?" And the answer was, "There you shall receive comfort for all your toil and joy for all your sorrow; you shall reap what you have sown—the fruit of all your prayers, tears, and sufferings for the King along the way. You shall wear crowns of gold and enjoy the constant sight of the Holy One, for 'there you shall see him as he is.' There also you shall serve continually, with praise, shouting, and thanksgiving, him whom you desired to serve in the world, though with much difficulty, because of the weakness of your flesh. There your eyes shall be delighted with seeing, and your ears with hearing the pleasant voice of the Mighty One. There you shall enjoy your friends again who have gone before you; and there you shall with joy receive every one who follows into the holy place after you. There you shall be clothed with glory and majesty, and shall ride out with the King of Glory. When he comes with the sound of trumpets in the clouds, as upon the wings of the wind, you shall come with him; and when he sits upon the throne of judgment, you shall sit beside him; and when he passes sentence upon all the workers of iniquity, be they angels or men, you shall have a voice in that judgment, because they were his enemies and yours. Also, when he returns to the city, you shall return too, with the sound of trumpets, and be with him forever."

Now as they drew near the gate, a company of the heavenly host came out to meet them; and the other two Shining Ones said to this company, "These are men who have loved our Lord when they were in the world, and who have left all for his holy name; and he has sent us to fetch them, and we have brought them thus far on their desired journey, so that they may go in and look their Redeemer in the face with joy." Then the heavenly host gave a great shout, saying, "Blessed are they which are called into the marriage supper of the Lamb."

At this time several of the King's trumpeters also came out to meet them; they were clothed in white and shining raiment and made even the heavens echo with their loud, melodious sounds. These trumpeters saluted Christian and Hopeful with ten thousand welcomes; and this they did with shouts and the sound of trumpets.

This done, they surrounded the two companions; some went before and some behind, some on the right hand and some on the left (to guard them through the upper regions); it was as if heaven itself had come down to meet them. Thus they walked on together. And as they walked, these trumpeters, by mixing their joyful and continual music with looks and gestures, signified to Christian and his brother how welcome they were into their company, and with what gladness they had come to meet them; and now the two men were in heaven before they even came to it, caught up in the sight of angels and the sounds of their melodious notes. They could see the city itself now, and they thought they heard all the bells ringing to welcome them. But above all were their warm and joyful thoughts about their own dwelling there, with such company, for ever and ever. What tongue or pen can express their glorious joy! And thus they came up to the gate.

Now when they reached the gate, they saw written over it in letters of gold, "Blessed are they that do his commandments, that they may have right to the tree of life, and may enter in through the gates into the city."

Then I saw in my dream that the Shining Men told them to call at the gate; and when they did, Enoch, Moses, Elijah, and others looked from above over the gate, to whom it was said, "These pilgrims have come from the City of Destruction because of their love for the King of this place." And then each of the pilgrims handed in his certificate, which he had received in the beginning; these were then carried in to the King, and when he had read them, he said, "Where are the men?" When he was told, "They are standing outside the gate," the King commanded that the gate be opened, "That the righteous nation," said he, "which keepeth the truth, may enter in."

Now I saw in my dream that Christian and Hopeful went through the gate; and as they entered, they were transfigured, and they had garments put on them that shone like gold. They were also given harps and crowns—the harps to praise and the crowns as tokens of honor. Then all the bells in the city rang again for joy, and they were told, "Enter ye into the joy of your Lord." I also heard the men themselves singing with a loud voice, "Blessing, honor, glory, and power, be to him that sitteth upon the throne, and to the Lamb, for ever and ever."

Now just as the gates were opened for the men, I looked in after them, and I saw that the city shone like the sun; the streets were paved with gold, and on them walked many men with crowns on their heads, palms in their hands, and golden harps with which to sing praises.

There were also those who had wings, and they answered one another without ceasing, saying, "Holy, holy, holy, is the Lord." And after that they shut the gates, and with what I had seen, I wished myself among them.

Now while I was gazing upon all these things, I turned my head to look back, and I saw Ignorance come up to the river; but he soon got across without half the difficulty which the other two men had encountered. For it happened that there was then in that place one called Vain-hope, a ferryman, who helped him over with his boat. So Ignorance ascended the hill to the gate, only he came alone, for no one met him with the least encouragement.

When he arrived at the gate, he looked up at the writing above it, and then he began to knock, assuming that he would quickly gain entrance. But the men who looked over the top of the gate asked, "Where did you come from?" and "What do you want?"

He answered, "I have eaten and have drunk in the presence of the King, and he has taught in our streets." Then they asked him for his certificate, so that they might show it to the King; so he fumbled in his coat for one, and found none.

Then they said, "Have you none?" And the man answered not a word. So they told the King, but he would not come down to see the man. Instead, he commanded the two Shining Ones, who had conducted Christian and Hopeful to the city, to go out and bind Ignorance hand and foot and take him away. Then they carried him through the air to the door that I had seen in the side of the hill and put him in there.

Then I realized that there was a way to hell even from the gates of heaven, as well as from the City of Destruction. And I awoke, and behold it was a dream.

THE CONCLUSION

Now, reader, I have told my dream to thee;
See if thou canst interpret it to me,
Or to thyself; or neighbor; but take heed
Of misinterpreting; for that, instead
Of doing good, will but thyself abuse:
By misinterpreting, evil ensues.

Take heed, also, that thou be not extreme,
In playing with the outside of my dream:
Nor let my figure or similitude
Put thee into a laughter or a feud.
Leave this for boys and fools; but as for thee,
Do thou the substance of my matter see.

Put by the curtains, look within my veil,
Turn up my metaphors, and do not fail,
There, if thou seekest them, such things to find,
As will be helpful to an honest mind.

What of my dross thou findest there, be bold
To throw away, but yet preserve the gold;
What if my gold be wrapped up in ore?
None throws away the apple for the core.
  But if thou shalt cast all away as vain,
I know not but 'twill make me dream again.

THE AUTHOR'S APOLOGY FOR HIS BOOK

When at the first I took my pen in hand
Thus for to write, I did not understand
That I at all should make a little book
In such a mode; nay, I had undertook
To make another; which, when almost done,
Before I was aware, I this begun.

And thus it was: I, writing of the way
And race of saints, in this our gospel day,
Fell suddenly into an allegory
About their journey, and the way to glory,
In more than twenty things which I set down.
This done, I twenty more had in my crown;
And they again began to multiply,
Like sparks that from the coals of fire do fly.
Nay, then, thought I, if that you breed so fast,
I'll put you by yourselves, lest you at last
Should prove ad infinitum, and eat out
The book that I already am about.

Well, so I did; but yet I did not think
To show to all the world my pen and ink

In such a mode; I only thought to make
I knew not what; nor did I undertake
Thereby to please my neighbor: no, not I;
I did it my own self to gratify.

Neither did I but vacant seasons spend
In this my scribble; nor did I intend
But to divert myself in doing this
From worser thoughts which make me do amiss.

Thus I set pen to paper with delight,
And quickly had my thoughts in black and white.
For, having now my method by the end,
Still as I pulled, it came; and so I penned
It down: until it came at last to be,
For length and breadth, the bigness which you see.

Well, when I had thus put mine ends together,
I showed them others, that I might see whether
They would condemn them, or them justify:
And some said, Let them live; some, Let them die;
Some said, John, print it; others said, Not so;
Some said, I might do good; others said, No.

Now was I in a strait, and did not see
Which was the best thing to be done by me:
At last I thought, Since you are thus divided,
I print it will, and so the case decided.

For, thought I, some, I see, would have it done,
Though others in that channel do not run:
To prove, then, who advised for the best,
Thus I thought fit to put it to the test.

I further thought, if now I did deny
Those that would have it, thus to gratify;

I did not know but hinder them I might
Of that which would to them be great delight.

For those which were not for its coming forth,
I said to them, Offend you I am loath,
Yet, since your brethren pleased with it be,
Forbear to judge till you do further see.

If that thou wilt not read, let it alone;
Some love the meat, some love to pick the bone.
Yea, that I might them better palliate,
I did too with them thus expostulate.

May I not write in such a style as this?
In such a method, too, and yet not miss
My end, thy good? Why may it not be done?
Dark clouds bring waters, when the bright bring
    none.

Yea, dark or bright, if they their silver drops
Cause to descend, the earth, by yielding crops,
Gives praise to both, and criticizes neither,
But treasures up the fruit they yield together;
Yea, so commixes both, that in her fruit
None can distinguish this from that: they suit
Her well when hungry; but, if she be full,
She spews out both, and makes their blessings null.

You see the ways the fisherman doth take
To catch the fish; what devices doth he make!
Behold! how he engageth all his wits;
Also his snares, lines, angles, hooks, and nets;
Yet fish there be, that neither hook, nor line,
Nor snare, nor net, nor device can make thine:
They must be groped for, and be tickled too,
Or they will not be catched, whate'er you do.

How doth the fowler seek to catch his game
By divers means! all which one cannot name:
His guns, his nets, his lime-twigs, light, and bell;
He creeps, he goes, he stands; yea, who can tell
Of all his postures? Yet there's none of these
Will make him master of what fowls he please.
Yea, he must pipe and whistle to catch this,
Yet, if he does so, that bird he will miss.

If that a pearl may in a toad's head dwell,
And may be found too in an oyster-shell;
If things that promise nothing do contain
What better is than gold; who will disdain,
That have an inkling of it, there to look
That they may find it? Now, my little book
(Though void of all these paintings that may make
It with this or the other man to take)
Is not without those things that do excel
What do in brave but empty notions dwell.

"Well, yet I am not fully satisfied,
That this your book will stand, when soundly tried."
Why, what's the matter? "It is dark." What though?
"But it is feigned." What of that? I trow
Some men, by feigned words, as dark as mine,
Make truth to spangle and its rays to shine.
"But they want solidness." Speak, man, thy mind.
"They drown the weak; metaphors make us blind."

Solidity, indeed, becomes the pen
Of him that writeth things divine to men;
But must I needs want solidness, because
By metaphors I speak? Were not God's laws,
His gospel laws, in olden times held forth
By types, shadows, and metaphors? Yet loath

Will any sober man be to find fault
With them, lest he be found for to assault
The highest wisdom. No, he rather stoops,
And seeks to find out what by pins and loops,
By calves and sheep, by heifers and by rams,
By birds and herbs, and by the blood of lambs,
God speaketh to him; and happy is he
That finds the light and grace that in them be.

Be not too forward, therefore, to conclude
That I lack solidness, that I am rude;
All things solid in show not solid be;
All things in parables despise not we,
Lest things most hurtful lightly we receive,
And things that good are, of our souls bereave.
My dark and cloudy words, they do but hold
The truth, as cabinets enclose the gold.

The prophets used much by metaphors
To set forth truth; yea, who so considers
Christ, his apostles too, shall plainly see,
That truths to this day in such garments be.

Am I afraid to say that holy writ,
Which for its style and phrase puts down all wit,
Is everywhere so full of all these things—
Dark figures, allegories. Yet there springs
From that same book that lustre, and those rays
Of light, that turn our darkest nights to days.

Come, let my carper to his life now look,
And find there darker lines than in my book
He findeth any; yea, and let him know,
That in his best things there are worse lines too.

May we but stand before impartial men,
To his poor one I dare adventure ten,
That they will take my meaning in these lines
Far better than his lies in silver shrines.
Come, truth, although in swaddling clouts, I find,
Informs the judgment, rectifies the mind;
Pleases the understanding, makes the will
Submit; the memory too it doth fill
With what doth our imaginations please;
Likewise it tends our troubles to appease.

Sound words, I know, Timothy is to use,
And old wives' fables he is to refuse;
But yet grave Paul him nowhere did forbid
The use of parables; in which lay hid
That gold, those pearls, and precious stones that were
Worth digging for, and that with greatest care.

Let me add one word more. O man of God,
Art thou offended? Dost thou wish I had
Put forth my matter in another dress?
Or that I had in things been more express?
Three things let me propound; then I submit
To those that are my betters, as is fit.

1. I find not that I am denied the use
Of this my method, so I no abuse
Put on the words, things, readers; or be rude
In handling figure or similitude,
In application; but, all that I may,
Seek the advance of truth this or that way.
Denied, did I say? Nay, I have leave
(Example too, and that from them that have
God better pleased, by their words or ways,
Than any man that breatheth now-a-days)

Thus to express my mind, thus to declare
Things unto thee that excellentest are.

2. I find that men (as high as trees) will write
Dialogue-wise; yet no man doth them slight
For writing so: indeed, if they abuse
Truth, cursed be they, and the craft they use
To that intent; but yet let truth be free
To make her sallies upon thee and me,
Which way it pleases God; for who knows how,
Better than he that taught us first to plough,
To guide our mind and pens for his design?
And he makes base things usher in divine.

3. I find that holy writ in many places
Hath semblance with this method, where the cases
Do call for one thing, to set forth another;
Use it I may, then, and yet nothing smother
Truth's golden beams: nay, but this method may
Make it cast forth its rays as light as day.

And now before I do put up my pen,
I'll show the profit of my book, and then
Commit both thee and it unto that Hand
That pulls the strong down, and makes weak ones
*   stand.*

This book it chalketh out before thine eyes
The man that seeks the everlasting prize;
It shows you whence he comes, whither he goes;
What he leaves undone, also what he does;
It also shows you how he runs and runs,
Till he unto the gate of glory comes.

It shows, too, who set out for life amain
As if the lasting crown they would obtain;
Here also you may see the reason why
They lose their labor, and like fools do die.

This book will make a traveller of thee,
If by its counsel thou wilt ruled be;
It will direct thee to the Holy Land,
If thou wilt its directions understand:
Yea, it will make the slothful active be;
The blind also delightful things to see.

Art thou for something rare and profitable?
Wouldest thou see a truth within a fable?
Art thou forgetful? Wouldest thou remember
From New Year's day to the last of December?
Then read my fancies; they will stick like burrs,
And may be, to the helpless, comforters.

This book is writ in such a dialect
As may the minds of listless men affect:
It seems a novelty, and yet contains
Nothing but sound and honest gospel strains.

Wouldest thou divert thyself from melancholy?
Wouldest thou be pleasant, yet be far from folly?
Wouldest thou read riddles, and their explanation?
Or else be drowned in thy contemplation?
Dost thou love picking meat? Or wouldest thou see
A man i' the clouds, and hear him speak to thee?
Wouldest thou be in a dream, and yet not sleep?
Or wouldest thou in a moment laugh and weep?

Wouldest thou lose thyself and catch no harm,
And find thyself again without a charm?
Wouldest read thyself, and read thou knowest not
  what,
And yet know whether thou art blest or not,
By reading the same lines? Oh, then come hither,
And lay my book, thy head, and heart together.

LIST OF SCRIPTURES CITED

Scriptures are listed in order of appearance.

Day 1: *The Light in a Dark Land*

Isaiah 6:5 NKJV   Matthew 4:16 NIV

Isaiah 9:2 NASB   Isaiah 60:1 NIV

Day 2: *"Nonsense!"*

Ephesians 4:18–19 NIV   Romans 12:9

Ephesians 2:4–5 NIV   John 10:10 NIV

Day 3: *You Call This "Happiness"?*

Isaiah 55:6–7

Day 4: *Floundering in the Swamp*

Psalm 119:105   Galatians 6:2

2 Timothy 3:16

Day 5: *"Why Throw Your Life Away?"*

Matthew 10:39   Proverbs 14:9

Proverbs 14:7   Proverbs 14:12

Day 6: *Shortcut to the Happy Life*
    Hebrews 12:18–21   Hebrews 12:28–29
    Hebrews 12:22

Day 7: *"Strait Is the Gate"*
    Matthew 7:13–14   John 13:35
    John 3:16, emphasis added

Day 8: *Knock, and It Shall Be Opened*
    Psalm 34:18   Ephesians 6:11
    John 8:44   Ephesians 6:16

Day 9: *Goodwill and Grace*
    John 1:14 NIV   2 Corinthians 12:9 NIV
    Titus 2:11 NIV   Hebrews 4:16

Day 10: *The Wiser Child*
    Romans 8:24–25 NIV   Romans 5:3–5 ESV

Day 11: *Fire, Oil, and the Devil*
    No citations

Day 12: *The Determined, the Despairing, and the Trembling*
    Romans 8:5–6

Day 13: *The Place of Deliverance*
    Romans 8:26   Romans 15:13 ESV

Day 14: *Prey for the Roaring Lion*
    1 Peter 5:8   1 Peter 5:9
    1 Peter 5:7

Day 15: *A Shortcut over the Wall*
James 4:8 NIV

Day 16: *Beasts of the Night*
Psalm 91:7   Hebrews 10:22–23 NIV
Psalm 90:10, 12   Psalm 32:11

Day 17: *Sharing His Stories*
1 John 1:2, 3   Hebrews 12:1–2

Day 18: *Pilgrims Born Beggars*
Philippians 4:6, 8   2 Corinthians 10:3–4

Day 19: *Equipping Pilgrim for Battle*
No citations

Day 20: *A Devilish Creature with Darts*
Luke 4:6–7   Ephesians 2:2
Luke 4:8   Ephesians 2:8
John 12:31   James 4:7–8

Day 21: *Hellish Rage*
Ephesians 6:10   Ephesians 6:16
Ephesians 6:11   Ephesians 6:17
Ephesians 6:14   Ephesians 6:11–12
Ephesians 6:15   Ephesians 6:18

Day 22: *Dragons and Blasphemies*
Hebrews 4:15   1 Corinthians 1:9
Mark 14:33–34

Day 23: *Darkness and Daybreak*
Psalm 23:4 KJV   Psalm 23:6
Psalm 23:4–5

Day 24: *Finding Faithful*
Proverbs 6:27–29, 32   Proverbs 5:18–19

Day 25: *Three Daughters*
1 Peter 1:3–4, 6   1 Peter 1:8–9

Day 26: *Shame: The Villain*
Romans 1:16   Matthew 22:37–39
Psalm 119:46

Day 27: *"A Devil at Home"*
Micah 6:8   Matthew 10:16

Day 28: *Vanity Fair*
1 Timothy 6:6, 8–9   1 Timothy 6:11–12
1 Timothy 6:10   1 Timothy 6:17

Day 29: *A Verdict of Guilty*
2 Timothy 1:7 NKJV

Day 30: *Silver-Slipper Religion*
Matthew 22:37   Romans 8:27
Romans 8:22–23   James 1:5

Day 31: *The Hill Called Lucre*

    Colossians 4:14   Psalm 16:11 GNT

    2 Timothy 4:10   Psalm 32:8

    Psalm 16:11 ESV   Jeremiah 6:16

Day 32: *Two Meadows*

    Proverbs 14:12

Day 33: *Giant Despair*

    1 Thessalonians 1:3   Ephesians 4:4

Day 34: *The Key Called Promise*

    Lamentations 3:18–19   Psalm 119:140

    Lamentations 2:21–22   2 Peter 1:3–4

    Lamentations 3:20–23

Day 35: *Seeing the Celestial City*

    Hebrews 13:8

Day 36: *Ignorance and Little-Faith*

    James 4:6–7   Psalm 51:17

    1 Peter 5:5   Matthew 23:12

    Psalm 18:27

Day 37: *The False Angel of Light*

    Jeremiah 33:3 NIV   Matthew 11:28

Day 38: *Beulah Land*

    John 14:2

Day 39: *Terror in the River*

Romans 5:15	2 Corinthians 1:2
Romans 5:17	John 6:40
Galatians 1:3	2 Thessalonians 2:16–17
Ephesians 1:2	

Day 40: *The Glorious Welcome*

John 17:24	1 Corinthians 2:9

About the Author

Harold Myra is an award-winning editor, author, and publishing executive. He served as the CEO of Christianity Today International for 32 years. He also taught writing and publishing at the Wheaton College Graduate School in Wheaton, Illinois. Harold is the author of several books, including *The Practice of the Presence of God: Experience the Spiritual Classic through 40 Days of Daily Devotion*. He and his wife, Jeanette, live in Wheaton, Illinois.

ALSO AVAILABLE

This special edition of Brother Lawrence's memoir presents an updated version of his classic text paralleled with a 40-day devotional by Harold Myra to help you focus on God and faithfully live in His presence.

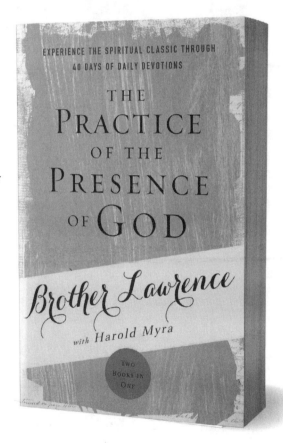

Discovery House.
from Our Daily Bread Ministries

dhp.org

Enjoy this book? Help us get the word out!

Share a link to the book or
mention it on social media

Write a review on your blog, on a retailer site,
or on our website (dhp.org)

Pick up another copy to share with someone

Recommend this book for your
church, book club, or small group

Follow Discovery House on
social media and join the discussion

Contact us to share your thoughts:

 @discoveryhouse    @DiscoveryHouse

Discovery House
P.O. Box 3566
Grand Rapids, MI 49501 USA

Phone: 1-800-653-8333
Email: books@dhp.org
Web: dhp.org